KEEP CALM
&
BECOME A KING

7 Simple Steps to take you from
Corporate Executive to **Entrepreneur**

How to free yourself from modern day slavery forever.

Sufian

Copyright © 2014 Sufian

All rights reserved. No part of this publication may be reproduced, stored in a retrieval system or transmitted in any form or by any means, electronic, mechanical, photocopying, recording or otherwise without the prior permission of the publishers.

First published in paperback in 2014

www.Sufian.me/KEEPCALM

ISBN-13: 978-1505258134

ISBN-10:1505258138

DEDICATION

This, my first book, is dedicated to my partner Nicola and our 3 beautiful boys, Harvey, Ashton and Sid.

ACKOWLEDGEMENTS

"In the land of the blind the one eyed man is King"; I found this not to be the case. In the land of the blind the one eyed man is viewed with scepticism and mistrust. The one eyed man needs to make or find his own Kingdom.

I would like to thank the many people that I have encountered so far on my journey form slave to King.

Almost without exception the people I have managed, worked for, employed, collaborated with and simply just met have been an inspiration and a constant source of learning.

Without all these people I would be left with just theories; so I thank you all for the gift that you have provided me with.

Some of the people I have encountered have just managed to work it all out for themselves, they are the fortunate ones. The vast majority, like me and you, try by trial and error and searching out great teachers to work it out.

Thank you.

This book is interactive. To access more content for free please visit www.**sufian.me/keepcalm**

CONTENTS

Introduction..6

Chapter 1: It's all about you.......................................12

Chapter 2: What's your business?.............................49

Chapter 3: Your new reality.......................................58

Chapter 4: The truth about staff................................85

Chapter 5: Life is not fair..115

Chapter 6: Cash is King..151

Chapter 7: Show me to the Exit...............................160

Introduction

"For £50m you can make me a slave *any time*". I'm shouting at the TV.

This was a number of years ago. I was watching a well-known singer describe himself as a slave to the record company that had signed him for a particular number of albums for a mind blowing sum of money. After a few years of great success he was reluctant to bend his artistic inclinations towards the demands of the record company and refused, amongst other things, to promote the latest album.

I didn't get it. I do now.

It is not about money, it is all about personal freedom to choose what you want to do, when you want to do it and with whom. When you are really free you become a King, not in the modern incarnation, but in a traditional sense. The ruler of all you survey, the ruler of your own destiny.

It is an uncomfortable truth that for all your efforts, rewards and material acquisitions that if you are employed then you are to some extent a slave. Someone has the power to tell you where to work, what time to work, how to dress, how much you will earn, when you can go on holiday, where you can live and who you spend the most of your time with. There are no physical bonds, but there are bonds nevertheless.

I saw the sting of this uncomfortable truth a few years ago. A friend of a friend had introduced me to a Director of a sizeable law firm. I had a product that I believed would be of benefit to them; some new technology.

This friend of a friend introduced me to the appropriate Director in the business and we arranged to meet at their Head Office. Charles was in his mid-thirties and had been promoted the previous year, his career was on fire. He told me this as we were having a coffee before the real reason for our meeting began.

After we had explored his background he asked me what I did, "what was it like being an entrepreneur?"

As I began explaining the freedom of choice that I had, to work with whom I wanted and when, I saw the first signs in his eyes. I continued and explained that with the summer holidays coming and the children having 6 weeks off that I would be taking the summer off too.

"Wouldn't we all like to do that?" Charles replied, half joking.

The potential sale was lost then and there, I knew it.

When the day had started Charles was a King, everyone around him agreed, friends, family and colleagues. He was doing great, a Director at such a young age. The future was full of promise and Charles was going to take full advantage of the opportunities that were ahead of him.

I had jolted his reality; I had questioned his success and the nature of his happiness. I had done this unwittingly; Charles had allowed my comments to impact on himself and his self-image.

Charles realised that he wasn't a King at all, he was a slave. Up until this moment a very happy and well paid slave.

The meeting continued and Charles decided not to take things any further. I would have done the same in his shoes. My company was small and there was a high degree of risk that Charles didn't need to take.

As far as I know Charles still works for the Law firm.

For some people being a slave might not be cause for concern, but, you are not "some people". The very fact that you have decided to read this book means that you are looking for a different path for yourself and exploring options.

You have always worked hard and applied yourself to whatever you have done. You could perhaps be described as a conformist.

You have a serious decision to make and unlike some other people you have something valuable at stake. You have something to lose. It is easy making choices when there are no alternatives worth considering. You have created these alternatives and created a dilemma for yourself. You have a career; you have something that other intelligent and hardworking people want.

The further and deeper you get into a career can result in it being more difficult, on a number of levels, to extricate you from this.

Maybe your career is not giving you the satisfaction that you seek or that you just require a new challenge or that something is just missing.

Whatever your motivation is, which we will cover in the first chapter, what you will get from this book is the opportunity to be introduced to the practical aspects of running your own business.

When I sat down to write this book I thought about instances that had resonated with me that I could remember over the past 30 years. Stories that people had relayed to me that I remembered. They were often the mistakes, the opportunity to learn. The success stories have their place but they tend to have less of an impact.

One of the goals is for you to have some insight, if you have never run your own business, of what it feels like to be a business owner or entrepreneur today. To get a mind's eye view from someone who has already gone down the path that you are contemplating.

You have made an investment in this book, congratulations and thank you. I am also giving away free various accompanying resources online to support this experience, for a number of reasons. Some of the material just lends itself to video or audio and I am also aware that we each have different learning preferences and styles.

I want you to be able to clearly think about this opportunity that you are considering and the next steps that you are going to take.

I want you to learn from the experiences of others who have had a similar experience and have messed up; this is their gift to you. This is my gift to you.

We can all react differently to the same stimulus and how you react is as individual and unique as you are.

You are about to be introduced to the world of the business owner and entrepreneur. What is not in the book is information that I know you can easily get elsewhere; how to write a business plan, the legal form your business should take etc. You are smart enough to work this out and seek out the appropriate professionals.

To get into the mind of an entrepreneur is one thing, to get into one that is a student of business is quite another, one that likes teaching and one who sincerely doesn't want you to go through the same pain, wasted time, stress and money that I've been through. I don't want anybody to go through that.

My hope is that as entrepreneurship and business ownership grows, as it inevitably will and people and organisations collaborate more and more aided by the growth of technology and the access to education to billions of people that this will bring serious change that will enhance the human experience.

Maybe you or someone who you inspire creates an innovation that makes a real difference to humanity, how great would that be? We've had centuries where access to capital and education were required for business success and now these barriers have be reduced to such an extent that they are now open to the majority of people, at least in Western democracies.

If you are not yet ready to learn much of this book will go in one ear and out the other. There is a saying "when you are ready to learn you will seek out a Teacher".

This book is for you if you are thinking about starting your own business or you have already started a business and realised that it is not delivering what you dreamed it would.

This book is for you if you are either well educated (degree level or equivalent) or have found yourself in a position of responsibility as a Team Leader, Head of Department, Head of a Division, Director, Managing Director or even a Chairman.

Why do I mention this? If you are looking for confirmation/affirmation that anyone can be successful and all you need is just hard work and that I will share stories of people who have achieved greatness even though they had no formal education etc. then this is not the place for you – please look elsewhere.

My own expertise and experience is that of someone who via a good education was able to make choices. I didn't have to start by running a market stall (not there is anything wrong with this and I have friends and family who have done very nicely from this).

My journey started in the corporate world and I moved from Senior Executive to Entrepreneur and I am now unemployable in the conventional sense.

My intention with this book is very clear; I want you to be in a position to make an effective decision as to the direction of your future with regard to starting and running your very own successful business.

Imagine we are sitting having a coffee and you have my undivided attention and I have your best interests at heart. The reason to think of it this way is that I want you to relax and see this as a personal discussion that is about the most important topic in the world to you – you and your future success.

My background has allowed me to work directly with thousands of employees and business owners both in large corporates and in smaller owner managed organisations. I have had the opportunity to look directly into their eyes as they have been able to articulate exactly what they really really want. This, as you will discover, is not as easy as one might assume.

To get the best out of this book I strongly suggest that you read the book in the order that is has been set out. At the end of the day you make your own decisions based on the advice that is provided. You can always come back and dip in and out for specific topics when you feel the need.

My experience is based in the UK and directly with a British workforce. The insights should resonate with anyone who lives and works in an established western democracy, but at the end of the day I will let you be the judge of that.

You will not find the practical advice that is in this book taught in any Colleges or Universities. You could spend years and a great deal of money and never become exposed to some of the experiences, solutions and perspectives contained in these pages.

Being a successful business owner is the best feeling in the world. You are truly taking control of your life and benefitting many others at the same time.

Your journey from being an Executive to Entrepreneur starts here; become a KING and throw away the shackles of slavery. The term King is interchangeable with Queen, but you knew that anyway.

I was compelled to take this journey when I started out 30 years ago, I just didn't know it.

If you feel compelled then this book is definitely for you.

> This book is interactive. To access more content for free please visit www.**sufian.me/keepcalm**

Chapter 1

Step 1: This chapter is about understanding and discovering who you are in the context of your desire to start your own business. What really motivates you, what are your strengths and how will you fill the inevitable "gaps"?

1.0 - The Intelligent Cabbage

For over 30 years I have been an active participant and student of the business world. To this day I dedicate a great deal of time each week to educating myself. I read books, attend seminars, webinars, watch online videos, buy courses, white papers, and follow interesting authors and authorities. *So what* I hear you say.

This is the point. You will have probably heard the 10,000 hours rule with regard to someone becoming a Master of something – the piano, violin, engineering, carpentry etc. This is only partly true (we would have to define Mastery); the truth is that being experienced is not a constant.

I subscribe to the view that the vast majority of jobs can "Mastered" in a very short period of time with the right application and the converse is true that 10,20 or 30,000 hours of experience can lead to a superficial understanding of any role with the person in question just doing sufficient to get by.

To illustrate the point I will describe my experience of working in an admin department of a food manufacturing business when I was undergoing training and working with a highly experienced Administrator who we will call Angela.

At this point I should state that any names and characters appearing in this work are fictitious. Any resemblance to real persons, living or dead is purely coincidental.

Angela had been with the company for over 35 years and she had a reputation of being quite a formidable character. She had become a Senior Administrator about 15 years before I met her.

On the first day with Angela she described how we received documents from the Despatch Department and then entered these onto the computer and then passed the documents onto the next department. I asked a few simple questions around where the documents came from. Why we were doing what we were doing? Where did the documents go to? What would happen if there was ever a problem with so and so? – You get the idea.

It emerged that Angela didn't know the answers to all the questions, so I took it upon myself to find out the ones where we had a gap. Now it turned out that in 35 years of working in the Admin Department that Angela had never been downstairs to where the products were made and where the Production, Despatch & Transport Departments were all situated – even though the paperwork she handled had some impact on each of these departments.

Angela told me that when she first joined she was supposed to have a tour of the factory, but, the Factory Manager was off sick, the tour was cancelled and it never got re-organised again.

I informed the local Managing Director and a factory tour was organised for Angela and some of her colleagues.

I learned a lesson about experience. You have to apply effort, talent and intelligence to it to make it truly meaningful.

If you send a cabbage on a world cruise with stops at various ports and interview the cabbage on its return you will find that whilst the cabbage had the experience of travelling the world its knowledge of geography is the same as when it started – zero!

Something about Me

Throughout my experience I have constantly asked questions, wanted to know why something was done, tried to work out simpler more efficient ways of doing things and most importantly tried to understand the people I came into contact with and tried to understand myself.

One of my bosses said "you make more mistakes than anyone I have ever met". He meant this as a compliment. He continued…"You also have more successes than anyone I have ever met".

He meant that I was not afraid to fail – I'm still not and I still make mistakes every day.

Some numbers about me, I have employed over 2000 staff, I have been responsible for over £1/4 Billion of turnover, trained over 3000 people – all whilst I worked in the corporate world.

As an entrepreneur I have generated more than £30m in sales, employed over 200 people and started successful companies from scratch and had a business failure.

I have been involved in traditional manufacturing, engineering, logistics, sales, marketing, project management, finance, IT and been Head of Divisions, Director, Managing Director, Chairman and Non-Exec Director.

My main interest these days are helping people to succeed by thinking clearly.

1.1 - Questions, Questions, Questions

The question we must first address is "Can anyone really start and run a successful business?"

Firstly, what do we mean by successful business? My definition is simple. A successful business is one that generates profits for you on an ongoing basis and does not require your day to day input.

This means that you go from being an employee to an employer. The vast majority of people who I meet that run their own business continue as employees, they just happen to work for themselves. They continue to trade their time for money and they end up seeing their dreams fade and become a distant memory. The reason why they started the business, with all the hopes of what it would mean to them and their family, becomes destroyed.

How could you achieve business success? There are a number of ways, firstly you could employ other people and trade their time for money. Secondly you could create some intellectual property and sell or license this. These days this could be as piece of software, an app, a book, a song or a design. The Internet has really been a game changer for the second option.

Think about the professions for a moment. Accountants & Solicitors typically sell their time for money. Solicitors do offer no win no fee, this is smart becomes it moves away from the time for money transaction. As a business owner you will pay for Solicitor's time.

Estate Agents, for all their faults, don't trade their time for money. They get paid on a percentage of the value of the house! This is pretty smart if you ask me.

There is a third route, for those of you are particularly risk averse, or don't believe that you can come up with a business idea (we will cover this in later chapters) and that is to buy a Franchise; a proven business model. If you are an entrepreneur you will shudder at the thought of this if this is your first business venture. You will not have the creativity and freedom; you will have someone else's creativity and systems to follow.

If Franchising is something that you are or have considered as a first step and the record of success for Franchisees as opposed to self-start-up businesses is undoubtedly better, then you probably are not an entrepreneur or you are holding back part of you because of either your uncertainty or fear of failure.

You might also just be better suited to this, the truth being that the "corporate you" is stronger than your entrepreneurial desire and inclinations.

The last option is to purchase a business, turn around a failing business or pick up a successful business at the right price. Large corporate businesses tend to have all the systems and procedures that are required to maintain the business year in and year out. This will probably not be the case with a small business. Often the owner will be directly linked to the identity and success of the business and therefore presents a major risk and obstacle to a sale.

I know many successful Consultants who will never be able to sell their business. It has no value when they retire. They have traded their time for money and customers expect to see them and only them, after all the business normally bears their name.

The facts are the facts. In the UK & in America around 80% of business start-ups fail in the first 5 years. A large number of the business owners that I have met have passed the 5 year mark but that doesn't mean that they are fine, far from it. In my experience the majority of the survivors are getting by and 80% of these will fail in the next 5 years.

There is another distinction I should make about business owners from the start. Not every business owner is an entrepreneur. **Some people run a business because it is just easier to do this than be employed**. Sometimes they cannot get a job; often they will work much longer hours than any employer could ask them to and for very little financial reward.

A couple of years ago I had personal discussions with around 500 small retailers who owned their own business. At a meeting with some of these retailers an observed said" I understand why they are called shop keepers now, they keep shop, and they are not business owners they just happen to own a business".

He, like me, was expecting them to be entrepreneurial, to be creative to try actively to attract customers, to solve problems, to take personal responsibility to have an energy that was infectious. He, like me, was disappointed.

The local high street is dying. I know one of the reasons why.

So a better question is **"Why do *you* want to start your own business?"** What will be different in a years' time? What will you have then that you don't have now? What won't you have in a year's time that you have now?

Get a piece of paper and a pen/pencil and write down the above questions. Write down your answers.

Why am I suggesting that you do this? I'll tell you, because if I was you I would be sceptical too. There will be nothing in this book that I haven't fully observed and believed in or I haven't researched to understand the *why* behind the words and actions.

I like being able to understand why I am doing something too. There is strong evidence that when we commit our thoughts down on paper with our own handwriting and not computer generated that there is a stronger connection and commitment associated with these actions. Scientists don't yet fully understand the how, and the why, perhaps they never will, but the research is clear, it makes a difference. Give it a try. Make a commitment to yourself, this is really really important.

Come back to paper in a day or so. Now when you read your reasons, your motivations what do you think. If someone you cared about came to you and told you these were the reasons why they wanted to start a business how would you react? Would you be supportive and convinced or would you try and talk them out of it?

Most people will start telling you that they have an idea for a business, they've seen a gap in the market, they've been inspired by so and so etc. This is the wrong place to start. Depending on how old you are and what experience and qualifications you have this decision to start a business could turn out to be irreversible. The "give it try, what have you got to lose" voices are just that, they are just sound. The voices that say "well you will never know if you don't give it a try" are speaking generalist platitudes that should make no difference to your decisions.

Take responsibility for your decisions and actions. Sometimes we all take risks, running your own business will always be a risk; however, I want you to mitigate the risk by following these steps before you decide to act. If you have already acted then perhaps you can still change course and receive the rewards your efforts deserve.

Am I trying to put you off? Absolutely I am.

Secondly, can anyone start and run a successful business?

I was at a barbecue a few years ago and a number of the people there ran their own successful businesses. One of the guys there was thinking about starting a business with his brother and he asked the very same question. "Can anyone run a successful business?"

Before I could answer, the following response was forthcoming.
"No, absolutely not. I know lots of people who should never, ever be let near running their own business. It would be a disaster for them."

The response came from a guy called Brian, who had run his business very successfully for over 20 years.

I asked him to elaborate. So he did.

"Running a business is stressful and difficult. You are constantly making decisions and everyone relies on you. I know many people who are terrible at making decisions and even more people who do not want to take any responsibility."

At the time I didn't fully agree with Brian, but that was a long time ago. I have the benefit of much more hindsight and insight now.

So, let me ask you a few more questions to help you.

Are you the type of person who despite being a modern day slave finds that the benefits far outweigh this one small negative? If this is you then you should probably stay where you are.

Are you the type of person that craves order and certainty? If this is you then again you should not being running your own business.

Are you the type of person who thinks that they could do a better job than their boss, that if you were in charge you would do this and that differently? Maybe it's been commented that you never switch off from work.

Are you constantly coming up with new and whacky ideas and angles on things, what I refer to as a crazy maker? If this is you then maybe starting your own business is the right decision for you.

Some really entrepreneurial people are great at starting businesses and awful at running them. A high degree of self-awareness means that to be successful they have no great difficulty putting in professional Managers.

If I had to describe an entrepreneur the first thing that would come to mind was their creativity and energy.

I did a talk to a roomful of entrepreneurs; there were about 100 people in the room. Due to the nature of the event these people were not business owners they were entrepreneurs.

I asked them to do the following:

1) Please raise your hand if you currently run your own business. About 80 of the people raised their hands.
2) Now lower your hands if you had not a single day off sick in the past twelve months.

After much giggling and chatting, everyone was trying to take a look around the room, there were no hands left up.

"We must have a special gene" I said. "If this room was full of employees the average number of days off for the year would have been around 9".

There could be a number of explanations for this. I like to think it is because entrepreneurs are by nature "can do" people and the joy of doing what you love every day adds to your general wellbeing.

Hopefully you are getting a feel for what it means to be an entrepreneur and what it means to be a business owner. Obviously business owners and entrepreneurs come in all shapes and sizes and the media is less than helpful in its depiction of the entrepreneur.

You could be forgiven for thinking that entrepreneurs are ruthless self-centred back stabbing, self-promoting bullies that would do almost anything to make a buck. On the other hand you could also believe that entrepreneurs know something, some secret that has passed the rest of humanity by. If only you could find out what this secret is you too could have the keys to the Kingdom and eternal happiness.

I can't speak for some of the two dimensional characters that the media delivers to us. All I know is that entrepreneurs are ordinary people with a particular set of skills. They are supportive, collaborative, willing to learn, energetic, risk taking, fault making, creative, inquisitive, questioning, dreaming, tenacious and above all impatient to make things better for others. They take action, they do things. They understand the 80/20 rule and that it applies to almost every situation.

Think about some of the people you know, think about their character. Think about someone who is not happy with their lot, their job, their pay, their partner, their looks or where they live. Now imagine that a new country was discovered in the middle of the Atlantic Ocean and the Worlds Governments had agreed that this new Country was going to be allowed to rule itself, a country with enormous amounts of natural resources and a temperate climate. This would be an opportunity to start a fresh, an America for the 21st century.

Think about your friend, given the offer of free passage and work would they go? Or would there be a million reasons why not to go.

What about you, what would you do?

This is not a challenge; there are no right or wrong answers. It is often easier to see in others that which we cannot readily perceive in our own character.

I am a big admirer of Albert Einstein and his famous capability to think about a problem and come up with possible creative solutions. He wasn't a laboratory physicist, he was a theoretical physicist. He was a great thinker. He apparently thought about one problem for over 10 years, now perish the thought, but there is inspiration to be had here.

His approach was very entrepreneurial. He could have been described as being indecisive or a day dreamer.

For every great character trait it is easy to provide an opposite and counter perspective. Let me give you some examples:

He is very straightforward *becomes* He is like a bull in a china shop

She is very decisive *becomes* She acts without thinking

He is very considered *becomes* He is bad at making decisions

The list could go on and on. I want you to think about how people may have described you in the past or would describe you now. I want you take ownership of how you decide to respond to these. Often people have a tendency to behave how people expect them to. We look for this, it's called a Confirmation Bias, and we do it without knowing that we are doing it. Even when you know that a particular confirmation bias exists, you still cannot stop yourself from succumbing to it from time to time.

When other people pass opinions about you they are really showing you their character, their beliefs and their limitations. This will become very important to understand and deal with if you embark upon starting your own business.

Whether you have overwhelming positive support to downright contempt and negative comments you will be the one dealing with this, this is your decision. Family and loved ones should be there to support you whatever your choices, however, I know many instances when this has not been the case.

There has never ever been a better time to start a business than right now. I mean right now, what is stopping you?

If you feel that you are almost ready but there is still some more research that you need to do or that you will wait until you've saved enough money or until you have your next foreign holiday then you are just procrastinating and continuing to deceive yourself. Act, and act now.

In the business world there is no such thing as perfect. I have some news for you, you are not perfect, and you know what, that's ok.

Think of some of the biggest companies and brands in the world, a technology company, we don't have to name any because even with almost unlimited resources they all publicly fail at some stage. These are the failures we get to hear and see, your failures will almost exclusively be confined to the corners of your mind and maybe a few other people.

Remember what my ex-boss used to say about me and I could deliver a thousand more examples (Thomas Edison with the light bulb) on the value of mistakes.

You are a King; failing is simply part of your journey to success.

1.2 - It's all about you

To put it another way, how well do you know you?

If I gave you a sheet of paper and asked you to write down what you don't like doing I'm sure it wouldn't take you long to fill it.

What you do like doing and what would motivate you to get out of bed every morning is a much deeper and more difficult question to answer.

Now here's the great thing, what I have discovered over the years is that the more difficult a question is the better your answers will be and therefore the resulting actions that you take.

In general people do not spend enough time thinking. Everyone is in a rush to get things done.

You have spent virtually all your life as a consumer not a creator.
Consuming is easy, you think you are making tough decisions and exercising your grey matter, but you are not.

I will talk about decision making at length in later chapters.

You are about to become a creator so that you can satisfy the needs and wants of consumers. Stop and think about this for a minute.

Look around you, from the clothes you are wearing to the chair that you are probably sitting on. These were all created by someone and in most case probably the process involved tens, hundreds, if not thousands of people to be able to satisfy the consumer, to satisfy you.

Now let's take a look at you and your role within your current organisation. You probably think that you are an expert in your chosen field maybe and that you are critical to the success of the organisation. If the organisation is large then the reality is that you are not critical to the success, you are simply a resource that the organisation consumes. You may have some creative input or you maybe the go to guy over all things technical.

Did you start the company? The answer is probably no, otherwise you would already have achieved your dreams and have levered other peoples labour and expertise for your ultimate benefit.

Corporate executives have a particular hurdle to overcome when starting a business. You thought you were a King; everyone around you gave you status. You worked hard and competed against other talented people and often won, you are a success.

Sounding great so far, but here's the rub. You never got to see the whole picture and even if you were Managing Director you could rely on a whole bunch of highly motivated professional and functional experts to take responsibility and support you.

No one starts a business really understating what it will be like, but my job is to paint the best picture I can for you so that you can avoid the pitfalls that the vast majority of people make, even the smart ones like you.

You have become maybe politically skilled at playing the game in order to succeed. In other words **you have learnt how to think and survive as a slave**. You are in a Kingdom of someone else's making and surrounded by many people who will love the Kingdom and feel really comfortable and safe being a modern day slave.

Virtually all the functions of a business are carried out by any organisation, irrespective of size. This means that when you start your business, forgive me for stating the obvious, you will have Sales, Marketing, Finance, Administration, IT, HR (if you have staff), Customer Service, and Purchasing departments at a minimum.

I now want to introduce you to Callum, Callum is an Engineering Director who is about to start his own business.

Callum has a passion for Engineering and he has designed the latest widget that he believes will revolutionise a particular industry. The majority of Callum's energy and focus is on the technical aspects of the business, after all get this wrong and there is no business, and also that's what Callum currently does.

Let's take a closer look. Callum has the option of redundancy, so he takes it. He was thinking of leaving and now he has the added bonus of some extra cash, he believes that world is conspiring to help him live his dream. He rents a small workshop, buys some of the latest design and manufacturing equipment and hires a part-time office administrator. Callum is a classic case of someone starting a business for all the right reasons and still not thinking things thru.

After a few months he has a prototype manufactured, in the end he had to approach a large firm to do this at no inconsiderable cost as his designed altered and he could not afford to purchase the correct machine at this time.

Now what does Callum do? He has never had to Market or Sell anything before and he is frightened and does not know where to start. He decides that he will recruit a Sales Representative. He finds out that the Sales Engineers are really hard to come by, the good ones, and that he just cannot afford the wages, so he takes on a less qualified and therefore less experienced and effective Sales representative.

Things go from bad to worse, the sales Representative is full of near misses and waiting for so and so to call back. During this time Callum is paying his wages, the rent for the workshop and the wages for the office administrator and there is no money coming in.

I don't need to continue because we can all see where this is heading. The point is this. Callum is intelligent, he is experienced, he is committed, he has cash to start the business and it is in an industry that he feels comfortable in and yet he fails. He fails because he failed to understand himself and the true nature of small business.

Virtually every business owner I have ever met started out focused on what they enjoyed doing, what their passion was. They didn't stop to think that this is just a very small part of running your own business.

Callum thought that he knew the industry; he did in terms of where large corporate engineering departments were concerned, however, he never worked in Sales, he never had to recruit anyone from scratch and he never worked for a small company, I could go on but I think you get the picture.

So before you have this light bulb moment of what you think your business should be, which we will cover later in the book, please try this exercise.

Get a sheet of paper and write out a company organisation chart for your new business. You will be the MD and to start off with you will be every other Head of Department unless you are starting out with a partner. Clearly identify in writing your strengths and weaknesses. How do you feel about dealing with customers? How will you Market & Sell your products/services? How organised are you when it comes to administration?

You will be drawn to some aspects like a magnet and feel comfortable whilst others will fill you with dread.

Doing this on paper is much safer and easier than waiting, like the Caullms of this world, to find out for real.

Armed with this information what can you do to address any gaps?

The reality is that **I have never met anyone, myself included, who has all the necessary skills and attributes to be able to successfully run their own business by themselves.** The range is too broad and too deep. We are also living through unprecedented times in terms of technological advances that are constantly altering the customer experience and market place.

Most businesses will outsource their accounts to Accountants; they will outsource legal work to Solicitors and their websites to Web Designers (more on this profession later in the book). The rest they normally keep, why?

Outsourcing might mean paying an employee, using a sub-contractor, collaborating and trading skills with another small business. Today there are more choices than ever, the thing is don't try and educate yourself on all aspects of the business that are not critical and even if they are critical if they are not within your skill set or area of motivation then it is always better to get someone else to do it.

You should not try to become a busy fool and constantly dabble in areas. Your real strength, whatever that is, is what you should concentrate on within your business. If you are great at personal relationships and awful at administration, get someone else to do it.

Running a small business is not like running a large company; there are inspirations that we can take, however, at the end of the day the lack of resources means that things just operate differently. Large companies often just get it wrong and it doesn't matter that much.

Every survey I have ever seen on how employees rate their bosses always comes out with the same results that the vast majority think that their bosses are doing a bad job. Again with my UK hat on I fully understand this, UK Managers in general are not trained adequately enough and even if they were it still would not make a great deal of difference to most of them because they, like most of the workforce, are probably in the wrong job.

The last appraisal I can remember having involved a discussion with my line manager about areas that I did well and areas that required "further development". What an utter waste of time, energy and resources.

It is hard enough trying to get out the skills that you have inside you and maximising these (let the great sales person spend all their time selling) rather than trying to "develop" skills that you don't have and in all reality for the role that you should be doing, you don't need.

So what about you, what are your strengths?

What do you really hate doing?

You should now to start to have a picture of who you are, what will be expected and waiting for you when you start your business and a different perspective on the world around you.

You are a King; always be true to yourself.

1.3 – Listen, do you want to know a secret?

Before I started a business I was reading biographies of famous business leaders and various self-help books on how to improve. Nothing wrong with this you might say; you might have been doing the same thing yourself.

My big mistake, and probably yours too, is that I was looking for an answer to a question that was just an awful question in the first place.

I wanted to know what the "secret" was. You know that little bit of information and insight that would turn my life around. Obviously, by some cruel twist of fate, this "secret" had eluded me. My answer was to work harder and search in more places in order to redress this oversight and gain the final piece of the jigsaw that would guarantee my success.

When I read a biography of a famous industrialist I truly believed that they had the "secret" and that they would share it with me, all I had to do was by the book and digest.

It finally dawned on me one day when I was in front of a group of refugees who wanted to start their own businesses. They were not what I expected. They were very well educated professionals who had often fled their country of birth, often under horrific circumstances. For one reason or another they found themselves in England and they were looking to try to rebuild their lives. The room was full of people with Masters Degrees and PhD's. Not youngster's either; they were nearly all middle aged.

I was explaining my story, how I became an Entrepreneur and then we had a question and answer session.

These sessions were facilitated by well-meaning people who had never run their own business, however, they were trying to educated and guide people in commerce and entrepreneurialism.

I was asked various questions and a couple of things dawned on me. Firstly, they expected help to start a business, financial help in particular and assumed that I had received this. My response was forthright. If you think you need a certain amount of money to start a business then what is stopping you from getting it; get off you backside and start earning. Wash cars, clean windows, work tables, deliver the mail, pick fruit etc. Why should someone else support your dream if you won't support it yourself?

The most important thing that happened was when a man asked a question about a biography he had just read on a famous British Billionaire.

He was a very earnest man; he was just a whisker away from figuring out how to become an entrepreneur he said, there was just one thing missing. He was going to buy another biography of some other celebrity industrialist and he was hoping to find the answer there. His question to me was could I suggest a biography to read or did I have the answer to his question, this one thing, this "secret" that was evading him.

I told him that I could save him the price of a book. I told him that if he wanted to become a fan of someone that was his choice. If he wanted inspiration that was fine, as long as he understood that was the reason he was investing time in reading this book or any other book.

The "secret" was not going to be found in any book. This "secret" was not going to be found because there isn't one, there never has been one and there never will be one.

Instead of spending time being a fan why not decide to become a student instead and learn from resources, material and people who you have decided will add to and support your journey and help you achieve your goals and objectives.

The other thing that you should do is work hard.

He looked at me as if I had just drowned a puppy or told him that Santa wasn't real.

I was questioning and trying to destroy his world view, who the hell did I think I was? I could see this in his eyes; he was just a few feet away.

I continued. The people that you are reading about have achieved something that you think that you want. Let us for a moment assume that this is true and that you are willing to live a life that resembles theirs. What are they telling you in the biography? They are telling you what happened to them, what choices they made, and what opportunities came their way, how they overcame adversity. They are not trying to teach you anything, this is not what they do. They understand that their celebrity will sell books. They understand that foolish people will by the book and hope that some of the "gold" of their success will rub off on the reader.

I don't play golf; I do know a lot of people who do. They buy the best equipment they can and they hope that in some bizarre way this will improve their game and maybe, just maybe they will be able to emulate the world's best players, their heroes.

There are no secrets and don't let anyone tell you that there are. Using the word secret is the same as using the words "short cut" or "the easy way".

The vast majority of really successful people are not concerned with or capable of teaching other people how to become successful. It is either not in their skill set as they probably don't understand it themselves or they just cannot be bothered, "explain to me again why I should do this?"

Don't become a fan and confuse this with being a student. There is a place for both; we all like to have heroes.

You are a King; you should also be a lifelong student.

Chapter 1.4 – The work-life myth

You will often hear people saying that they want to start their own business because they want a better work-life balance. This assumes that in their understanding their current balance is out of whack.

If you watch the faces of experienced business owners, as they listen to this, you would see wry smiles and comments of "Good luck with that one".

These experienced business owners believe that it is quite the opposite when you start a business and that you have to sacrifice your life to make the business work.

Let me attempt to break down this myth by explaining a different approach and a different truth.

First of all the saying "work-life balance" is just erroneous. This assumes that we have work on one side of the see saw and life on the other. It fools us into making a distinction between work and life as if the two were somehow separate, a world where work is "bad" and life is "good". A world where work is something you have to do and life is the real you, the things that you really want to do.

At the end of the day they share one common aspect and that is that whether you label things to do as work or life they are all just "things to do."

You and I have "things to do" and we have a finite amount of time. This is the first part of debunking work-life balance myth.

The second part is the prevailing wisdom from people who have had the experience that you are about to embark upon. The reality is that from a distance this might look as though you are about to share the same experience but on greater scrutiny as we get closer we realise that this just isn't the case.

They jumped into this experience without your preparation and awareness, they fell into the same traps as the majority of people and they now view the experience as common and inevitable. They have to see it this way otherwise they have to admit they got it terribly wrong; some of them will even take pride a sort of badge of honour that they went 2 years without seeing their

children or being home before 10pm.
Imagine we were having a discussion with Picasso, the painter just in case there are any celebrities I'm not aware of with the same name, and we asked him how he managed his work life balance. What do you think his response would be?

It would be an alien concept, make it an alien concept for you.

You are the King in everything you decide to do.

Chapter 1.5 – Crimes of passion

"Do I have to be passionate about my business?" is a question that often gets asked.

The answer to this is yes and no.

It is too simplistic a question to be meaningful and can therefore cause confusion when trying to work out your answer.

You will hear people telling you that passion is a key ingredient, that with passion it will not feel like "work" at all and because of this you have a much greater chance of success. This passion that you have will be felt by everyone, employees, suppliers and most importantly customers.

There are 3 main areas of a business that you can be passionate about. These are **PROCESS, PRODUCT & PEOPLE**.

Let's look at Process first. If you have worked for a large organisation and really enjoyed your job then you probably enjoyed the process, at least your part that the organisation allowed you to carry out.

You might have thought to yourself that the actual product or service that was being delivered was almost immaterial. "We could be selling baked beans or insurance, it doesn't really matter".

It is possible that you never came into contact with the product or service.

If this describes you then you need to consider this in deciding what your business will be. On the surface of it you have the biggest possibility of success as all businesses will have a process; however, will you be passionate about this?

To some extent this describes me. I love the process of creation within a business and being able to bring products and services to market, however, there are certain processes with some businesses that I could think of that just do not turn me on.

The thought of any type of catering or food serving just doesn't appeal to me at all, if I had talents as a creative Chef perhaps it would but I don't.

So the process for me also includes variety, to stop me from getting bored.

Take a quick look at the music industry. There are some performers or bands that have written songs decades ago and are satisfied with playing these songs night after night for years. This would be my idea of hell.

There are other artists who continually want to move on and create something new and experiment all the time.

The second passion is Product.

You may be very passionate about a particular product or service. You will definitely meet people like this and sometimes their passion for the product can boil over into the realms of being a zealot, which can be overpowering and off putting.

If you have created your own product that you have been working on for years, or you are convinced this new thing will change the world then this might be you.

Someone may have introduced you to a new product or service or concept and you are 100% sold on this. You can only see the upside and you are raring to go. You have it all worked out as to why this product is the best thing ever and you spend every waking moment thinking about this.

When you worked for a large corporation it is possible that you were passionate about the product or services they provided but I doubt that it was the primary reason for you joining them.

Your passion for the product might mean that the process within your business is less of interest to you, you might even be quite happy to outsource most of this.

Think of an architect, they have grand plans for an iconic building; this is their passionate product, more precisely the design of the building is. For their dream to become a reality they have to outsource virtually all of the activity to make their dream come true.

Hopefully you are beginning to realise that what you are passionate about should have huge implications for what business you choose and how you decide to operate this business.

The last passion is People. By People I mean customers, the people who will interact, use and benefit from your products and services.

This is the area where you will see most written about passion with regard to running your own business, after all without customers businesses do not exist.

You may want to improve a particular aspect of people's lives or deliver a better experience than they currently get from other products and services in the market place.

The customer is central to your thoughts; you are constantly trying to look at things from their perspective. You are continually refining your offer, getting feedback and engaging with existing and potential customers.

You are connected to customers via social media, if this appropriate; your mantra is that if you keep close to your customers and understand them you will always be able to serve them.

There are people that I know who are very successful, in terms of financial reward, who do not have a passion for the Process, the Product or the People. One person I know just has a passion for doing a deal, buying a company and then selling it for a higher price; I suppose thinking about it this is his process.

It is easy to make a mistake that a hobby that you are passionate about will make a great business for you and that this will be your vocation. Sometimes we have a hobby that takes us away from our normal day to day activities, sometimes a hobby allows us to express part of ourselves that we wouldn't otherwise access.

There are many people who have pursued the road to converting their hobby into a business and ended up destroying the love they had for the hobby in the first place, a definite lose lose scenario.

It might not be obvious to you what your passion is, you might never have thought about it before. You really must start to think about it now. We tend to enjoy the things that we are good at, so this might be a good place to start if you are struggling with this.

Any business that you are thinking about starting will have processes, products and people. Write down what these are and describe what is involved with each of them and ask yourself whether you are particularly drawn to any of them, sometimes it will be blindingly obvious.

You are designing your own Kingdom, this takes thought and consideration.

You are the King; don't fall into the trap and commit a crime of passion.

> This book is interactive. To access more content for free please visit www.**sufian.me/keepcalm**

Chapter 1.6 – Being Dumb is the new Smart

One of the problems with having a brain is that you have a tendency to use it. You can see various options and opportunities. You can be creative and create solutions.

Let us imagine for a moment that you are not smart, my belief is that if you were not smart that this would dramatically increase your chances of success as an entrepreneur.

I know that it sounds counter intuitive, but let me take you on a short journey, you will need your brain for this, and I will prove to you that being Smart is a distinct disadvantage.

In the Corporate world of slavery your brain helps you enormously because you are in small pool where intelligence is normally valued.

Now obviously I am not going to ask you to undergo an operation that will relieve you of millions of brain cells and I still want you to retain your intelligence, I just need you to pretend that you don't have it for a while.

Think about a million people who will start their own business today. Now imagine that within 5 years 800,000 of these people no longer have their business. They have lost money, time and their dreams of making a better life for themselves, their family and enriching the experiences of many customers.

Stop and think about this for a moment. Some of these people gave up, by choice, well paid jobs with stability, status etc. and took the plunge. Why? The answers, as there is not one answer, are varied. Who knows what motivates another person, it is difficult enough finding out what motivates you.

Why do you think that they have failed? What do you think contributed to this failure? Were all the failures a particular type of person?

Let's explore the possible reasons together.

They failed because they didn't work hard enough. Do you *really* believe this? Think about it. 800,000 people didn't succeed because they didn't work hard enough. If you think this is true you are wrong. If success as an entrepreneur was about hard work then the success rate in the first 5 years would be 99%.

These people started out with their dream, they wanted to make a difference. They were going to give up well paid jobs and careers, invest their life saving s and maybe that of some of their friends and family and then simply didn't work hard enough. Obviously the answer cannot be that they didn't work hard enough.

They failed because they weren't sufficiently formally educated. I know you don't believe this. Almost at every turn everyone else is telling you that anyone can become an entrepreneur. You may have met some or indeed read about or seen some in the media, you already know that some of these people are not very bright and not well educated. This didn't stop them becoming successful and it didn't prevent some very bright people from failing.

They failed because…. You fill in the blanks. There has to be something that connects these people otherwise how can we learn from this?

The focus is on who these people are. The truth is, this is an uncomfortable truth for those of us who are Smart, and that they failed because of what they did, not who they are.

I'll say this again, they failed because of what they did and NOT because of who they are.

Another way of saying this is "It is what you do that really matters".

How does this relate to being Smart? The chances are this makes you feel uncomfortable because of the connotations of this. You only feel uncomfortable because you are Smart.

In your head you are probably translating the information this way. "If it doesn't matter who I am then what is the point in having all this talent?"

Perhaps you might even be thinking that this is not for you or that I don't know what I'm talking about. Neither of these is probably true.

You are an individual and you want to express yourself, you want your personality to come out via your business. I am not suggesting for one minute that it shouldn't.

The trouble with Smart people is that you want to try and the bend the world so that it resembles what you think it should be like rather than what it is really like. In the real world of business there is no sense of fairness. The people who you believe should prevail and succeed often don't and the ones that you see has having no redeeming features at all can often succeed.

If you weren't Smart none of this would matter, you might not even be aware of it. You would simply accept that it is what you do that matters and not who you are. You would accept that it is the world as it is rather than the way you think it should be.

Just because you are Smarter, more creative, more genuine, harder working than the next guy doesn't mean you have any better chance of succeeding in running your own business, in fact it probably means the exact opposite.

Business is very simple. Next time you are out in a crowd take a look around you. These are the people, some of them at least, who will buy your products if you are successful. What do they look like to you? What do you think you know about them?

A less Smart person is shown that there is a simple way to act to run business and they don't have the distractions that you have. They are not constantly kept awake at night by thinking up new creative business ideas, they do not worry themselves with a million what if scenarios. They act and accept that their actions have consequences.

If you weren't as smart you could do the same. You could free yourself from your incorrect beliefs that YOU will make a profound difference to the business you are about to run. The reality is that YOUR ACTIONS will make the biggest difference.

So do yourself a favour please, be Dumb for a while and accept that it is what you do that matters the most and NOT who you are.

Chapter 1.7 – There's nothing wrong with perfect

If we continue to think about what you do that matters let's turn our attention to the "what".

The biggest delaying factor in people starting to run a business or when they have started a business to taking action is the desire for perfection.

There are millions of distractions out there seemingly designed to divert us from our real cause. Our brains are wonderful at seeking these out at the most inopportune moment.

There is no such thing as perfection in business and absolutely no room for a perfectionist.

If you try and dot every "i" and cross every "t" you will never take any action.

If you want to draw a "pig" on a sheet of paper, almost irrespective of your skill or lack of drawing skills, and your goal is that someone else recognises this as a pig how long would this take you?

You have achieved your goal in a few seconds. You could convince yourself that you do a better job, start again, add some colour, use coloured pencils, no use paint etc.

This is such an easy and convenient trap to fall into.

I was in San Francisco walking around the shops a few years ago. There was a large retailer that was having a refurbishment. All the walls were taken back to the reveal the bare brickwork underneath. The shop kept open whilst the scaffolding was outside and had signs up apologising for the disruption but also asking customers what they thought the new interior should look like. They had that many comments that the interior looked great as it was that they decided to keep it that way.

They listened to their customers, saved a heap of money and above all acted. A perfectionist in charge would have closed the store and spent a fortune on re-decorating the interior and for what benefit to the business and its customers?

No business is perfect; no business will ever be perfect. Get 80% of the way and implement, now. What are you waiting for?

Because you are Smart, you will ask yourself all sorts of questions that in the short term are irrelevant to the success of your business. What if a customer buys this and then changes their mind and does this, can we have an automated system to handle this?

Yes you can, it will cost a fortune and delay you by months and will not begin to tell you whether you have a successful business or not. You can answer the question when you having thousands of paying customers, or when the instances arise and you have to deal with it then.

You are a King; act now.

Chapter 1.8 – It's now or never

You have completed your preparation and research. You have tried as best as you can to understand yourself, what motivates you and you have decided upon a business that meets your needs, at least in theory.

As you enter this next phase of your journey and your personal development you will be faced with new, fresh and exciting challenges and numerous decisions.

For a moment let us explore the difference between choices and decisions, as people often confuse the two.

You made a choice to start a business. This is a major turning point in your life, a watershed moment that will lead to the need to make decisions that you would not have been confronted with otherwise.

Spending real quality time on the choices that you make is critical for your success and happiness.

The day to day decisions you make, whilst they might be difficult and have far reaching consequences only came about in your business because of the choices you made.

This next chapter will help you prepare for the decisions you may have to make given the choices you have decided upon.

Chapter 1.9 – If at first you don't succeed….

You finished off the sentence. We all do. If at first you don't succeed try, try and try again.

This mantra will be around you everywhere. It will be in your head.

You will hear people tell you their stories of how they rang a prospective customer 27 times and eventually got that meeting that led to a great big order.

It is there to inspire you, to motivate you and to let you know that you know that you should never quit. Success is just 3 feet away.

This mantra re-enforces one of the most dangerous aspects of our psyche and that is that **you don't deserve success yet unless you have worked hard enough for it and suffered**. If you get success straight away you were probably just lucky and therefore undeserving.

The mantra also plays to the masses, the people with no or very little talent. It could be you; all you have to do is work hard. Does this sound familiar?

I don't do the lottery. I don't hope that some random piece of good financial fortune will land in my lap. I don't cloud my mind with the "what if" questions associated with such a windfall.

We've already explored the fact that if hard work was the main quality that small business owners needed then the vast majority would prosper and we know that this is not the case.

What if you subscribe to a different mantra, a different perspective on your approach to business?

"**Insanity**: doing the same thing over and over again and expecting different results." *Albert Einstein*

Stop and think about this. The vast majority of business owners out there are getting it wrong. The advice they are getting is wrong, the choices that they have made are wrong. The decisions that they are making are wrong.

Fundamentally what they are doing is wrong.

Your task is simple. You are smart. Your task is to do what is right for you and your business. Will you get it right first time? Probably not.

Will you continue blindly doing the same thing in the hope that you will win the lottery? Absolutely not.

How will you know when to change direction or try something new? This is a decision you will have to make alone. It will depend on so many different variables, not least your ability to make effective judgement calls.

You are the King; learn quickly from your mistakes, they are your friends.

Chapter 1.10 – Shiny object syndrome

This is linked in a way to Marketing Plumbers (see Chapter 3.9) just because sometimes Marketing Plumbers appear bearing gifts that are shiny objects.

If you were dumb these shiny objects wouldn't interest you and you wouldn't attract them. The fact that you are smart and get easily bored is the problem.

You always want to explore and improve your knowledge and shiny objects well they're shiny and new.

They come in endless shapes and sizes and are a constant distraction.

Someone is trying to be helpful and suggests that this might be of interest to you. They do not have your filters in place (I will discuss this next) they are still overwhelmed by the world and think that they might be helping you.

Someone else has a problem, you love solving problems. "Could you just have a look at this for me?, you're good at stuff like this."

My answer used to be always yes, now it is invariably no. Make your stock answer no.

If you find the shiny object syndrome to be debilitating you and your business then you are probably going to derail your business.

You are the King, make a decision, and just say "no".

Chapter 1.11 – Does that thing come with a filter?

I tried for years to "get myself organised". I would spring clean my desk, files and folders every now and then. I would read books on how to become more effective at time management.

None of this made any difference, because I wasn't striking at the root cause of the problem, I was always dealing with a symptom.

Some people like dealing with symptoms all the time because it makes them feel comfortable and wanted.

I worked with a Manager once; we'll call him Derek, a very nice guy. All of Derek's staff thought that he was a good Manager, he cared about his staff. I ran a team of the same size in the same part of the country, doing exactly the same tasks as Derek's team.

I observed Derek, I was cherry picking as a young Manager to see what I could learn from him. I watched as he interacted with his team, he was visibly happy. He was in his word, "solving a problem" for his team and they appreciated him for it.

My team didn't need this problem solving because the symptoms never occurred, once I had addressed the root cause.

I used to call Derek a sticking plaster Manager; he would walk around all day with a bunch of plasters (band aids) in his pocket. Every now and then someone would appear with a cut finger and Derek would offer a sticking plaster, the problem solved.

Derek had been doing this for over 20 years now. I had been there 4 weeks and emptied my pockets of sticking plasters.

What Derek never investigated is why these people had cuts on their fingers, it never occurred to him find out. It turns out that there was a man in the next room with a blunt knife who kept on accidently cutting people. I took the knife off him, the cuts stopped and the sticking plasters weren't needed anymore.

Back to my organisational problem, I was trying to get myself organised because on occasions I was getting overwhelmed and felt that I just couldn't cope with the amount of workload, and every piece of new technology just made it worse.

One day I heard someone ask these questions.

"When you were a child did you ever visit a large Library?"

I answered the question even though it wasn't addressed to me. Yes I had visited a large Library in the centre of town.

"Were you overwhelmed when you went inside? After all the shelves were full of books, thousands of books on the widest range of topics imaginable."

No I wasn't overwhelmed.

"Why were you not overwhelmed? I will tell you, it was because you had gone to the Library to find a particular book on a particular topic. You had a filter in place".

The clouds parted and I saw clearly that this is why I was always struggling to get on top of my daily workload. I didn't have sufficient filters in place.

Added to this I understood too that your brain does not work like a priority list. It can only deal with things that need to be done; as a consequence the things that you still need to do that are vital are given the same status, at least by your sub-conscious, as the minor things that are not urgent and you will get around to one day.

I acted and started to look at what my priorities were what actions stemmed from these and then re-arranged my activities. I was left with a sorting process and the ditching of well over 50% of the things that used to clutter my in box, to do list and my sub-conscious.

This worked, I had failed every other time as I always started from the bottom, on the things I was currently doing rather than looking at things from a more global perspective. Today I have the correct filters in place and this has made an enormous difference to my working life.

Chapter 2
Step 2: Following on from your findings in Chapter 1 we now take a look at what business you want to start and clearly consider the implications that are associated with your choice.

Chapter 2.0 – What's the Big Idea?

The Big Idea is where most people start. If you mention to anyone that you are thinking about starting a business the first thing they will ask you is "what" the business is about.

It is the wrong question to ask and to answer when there are so many more meaningful and interesting questions.

As you explain to friends and family, with all this enthusiasm that is bursting through you, you will analyse every facial response pleading for approval and consoling yourself, when the response is less than enthusiastic, that it requires some further work.

We live in a world where everyone is a critic. It is easy to criticise and difficult, very difficult to create.

Give someone a blank sheet of paper and ask them to write down what they think you should do or the organisation you work for should do and the average person will hand back a blank sheet of paper.

Now try the exercise with the same people and put some ideas in front of them and now see how they rise to the challenge with gusto.

Behind the question of what is your business about are the real questions in disguise. The real questions are "Why?"

Why are you deciding to this?
Why do you think this will work?
Why do you think people will buy this?
Why do you think that there is not already a product/service like this?
Why don't you wait a while?
Why now?

The only question that really matters at first is **why** you want to do this?

Your motivation, your reason for doing this will be the single biggest determinant of the whether this new venture will be a success or not. It is therefore vital that you spend time answering this question and answering the question honestly.

Let me help you with some of the answers that I have received when I have asked this question:

Why do you want to start a business?

I want to be rich. I have seen (XYZ) and they are driving a great car, have a wonderful house and if they can do it then so can I.

I want to be my own boss. I don't like anyone telling me what to do.

I want to work fewer hours and strike a better work-life balance.

I love doing this as a hobby and just thought that if I could turn this into a full-time thing that this would be great.

I'm full of ideas and these days all you need is a great idea and in a few years I could be as big as (Facebook, Google, and Twitter etc.)

I've had this idea for a new product/service for a while and I'm convinced that it will sell and if I don't do it now I will kick myself.

I have been made redundant numerous times and I am looking at security for me and my family.

I am approaching forty and realise that my career options are closing down.

The above examples all have one thing in common. They are all centred on the people starting the business themselves and what it means to them.

This is highly unlikely to work. The "Why" should relate to customers and what it means to them, after all without any customers you will not be able to achieve any of your goals and aspirations.

Chapter 2.1 – Wow, that's an ugly baby

Having decided what your business will be about you now begin to tell people about it, at first with friends and family. You may need to raise some money from them or you maybe just want to share your great news.

People who love you and like you and care about you are in general the least dispassionate when it comes to assessing any business ideas that you may have.

Friends and family will generally tell you what a great idea this is, if they are investing money with you, they will want to be positive and they will be sharing your dream with you.

If you've ever seen any of those Reality TV singing programmes where a contestant is genuinely shocked to find out that the professional judges believe that they cannot sing, you know what is coming next.

They defend themselves and recount how their friends and family tell them that they have a beautiful voice, how they sound like an angel. The judges must be wrong; they must have something wrong with their ears.

Now the Producers of these shows have something to answer for, this type of car crash TV is both cruel and yet at the same time you are left as a viewer thinking "What were they thinking of, they MUST have known that they could not sing".

It made for good TV, something to talk about at the expense of the deluded singer.

Your business idea will be your baby, your friends and family will tell how beautiful your baby is. The first time you expose your baby to an outsider, someone who is dispassionate, they might potentially tell you that your baby is ugly.

How will you deal with this and what, if anything, does it mean?

Testing your ideas before you go to market and before you make large irreversible decisions is a gift. Asking your potential customers about your product/service idea is vital. There are many ways that you can do this. The feedbacks will either support the directions you are heading in or let you know clearly that something is fundamentally wrong. If you have an ugly baby it is better that you find out about it now so that you can do something about it.

Chapter 2.2 – You take the high road

So you are clear that you have the particular qualities to start a business, you have questioned your own motivation and understood what theoretically lies ahead and have some strategies ready to deal with these.

What will your business be?

To make this easier for you I am going to give you only 2 possible choices.

Firstly, a business that already exists, people already understand it and you have decided to offer something new/different that will meet the needs/desires of potential customers.

Secondly, a new idea, that will revolutionize a particular market/industry and deliver a new experience for customers.

Let me expand a little.

The first business will attract existing customers, however, the market is already very competitive and the big question is how will you establish yourself as being different?

The new idea has no obvious competition, you are creating a new market, and in theory you could charge what you wanted.

Based on the above positioning statements which business would you go for?

People think that they have to come up with a new idea or invention. This is where the money is. This is what being an Entrepreneur is about. How wrong they are.

Think about it. You have developed a product/service that no one has ever seen before. Your first task is to persuade and convince people that they need this in their lives. This will take up a great deal of energy and potentially a great deal of money in bringing your new idea to market.

I met an inventor a few years ago. He had spent his life savings on trying to protect his invention from being copied. He had Patents all over the world.

He had lost his house, his career and he came to me to discuss raising some additional funds. His inventions, there were a small number of them, seemed to be very interesting and potentially very lucrative.

He had his business for almost a decade and during this period it transpired that he had not made a single sale. I wished him well, after a couple of meetings.

Starting a business is difficult, so why would you handicap yourself by wanting to try to introduce a new concept?

If 80% of businesses fail in the first five years, you can probably say that new (innovative) product failures would reach 99.9%.

There is a TV Show in the UK called Dragon's Den. The concept is simple. A person (or persons) with a new business idea has the opportunity to pitch a small number of successful entrepreneurs for money in return for a stake in their fledgling business.

All the people who pitch have had a new idea. None of The Dragons made their money from new ideas. Their wealth came from established markets and products. What they have is celebrity and access to contacts that their success has afforded them. They have no crystal ball or particular set of gifts to distinguish one idea above another. It is prime time pantomime. The trouble is that some people now think that you have to have a new idea to make it, to start a business. I know this because I recently visited numerous Universities in the UK and spoke to literally thousands of students.

At all costs, try to avoid a new product in a new market. You may be the exception and be the exception to the rule.

If you have just read the above and are getting hot under the collar and are convinced that you have the next big thing, I am genuinely pleased for you, however, the chances are you are wrong and you are deluded.

If you want to seek comfort in the story of one person who against all odds successfully launched product X and is now a Billionaire, please go ahead. My role here is not to dampen your dreams; however, I could give you better odds on winning the National Lottery (which currently stand at 14 million to 1 in the UK) and all you would potentially lose is £1.

The fact that someone won the Lottery just means that they were lucky. You cannot re-create their luck; you cannot model it, you can only watch from a distance and make your own conclusions.

The vast majority of innovations come from small businesses, not large ones. The large businesses just tend to buy up the smaller ones and consume them and lever their innovative products/services.

Why do you have a much better chance with an existing market and trying an innovation that offers something new?

Let's start with the obvious. There are already people buying the product. You are not trying to convince or educate them.

Secondly, you can analyse what the current offerings are. You can even experience them for yourself. These days you can easily find out on line what people are particularly unhappy about and look at creating a solution for this.

You are the King; choose which path to take after considering all your options.

This book is interactive. To access more content for free please visit www.**sufian.me**/keepcalm

Chapter 2.3 – By accident or by design

You've chosen the industry sector and products/services that you think that you want to offer.

Now let's take a closer look before you commit yourself, after all this decision will impact you virtually every day for the next few years at least.

You have looked at other similar businesses and maybe you are building your own business in their image, before you do we should consider the options open to you.

To illustrate this point we will follow the journey of Joe and the choices he has available to him.

Joe has decided to take voluntary redundancy; he currently works as Head of Customer Services.

Joe has seen the rise of jobs being shipped abroad to cheaper sources of labour on the international market. These jobs would be considered "white collar" and in some cases professional jobs.

The growth of emerging world economies and the rise of technology have meant that once secure jobs are now potentially in danger.

Joe has spent the last few years interviewing highly qualified graduates who are seeking out tele-sale or customer service roles in order to get on the career ladder. Jobs for which they are over qualified for, but a job is a job.

Joe thinks he has seen the writing on the wall and he now has an opportunity to act.

His view is quite simple and yet quite compelling.

If someone is physically required to be in attendance at a customer's premises then this particular job cannot be outsourced overseas.

He plans to spend some of his redundancy re-training to become a plumber and run his own business. He feels that the customer service levels within this industry sector are so low that he cannot fail to succeed if he works hard, is technically competent and has the customer at the centre of his plans.

Whilst he completes his training, which he started part-time a couple of years earlier, Joe has been thinking about how to operate as a plumber and talking to lots of self-employed (owner manager) plumbers.

Where Joe lives there are a shortage of Plumbers and everyone he speaks to have no great difficulty getting work.

Joe has been looking at the sacrifices that running a traditional Plumbing business would mean and it is a price he is not willing to pay.

Joe has two small children and enjoys spending quality time with them and his partner. He hates the term lifestyle business; he is ambitious however and he has no desire to create a major conflict between a choice he can make and the life he currently really values.

If Joe decides to follow the path of a typical Plumber he is aware that he will tender for jobs, installing a new bathroom for example, and that he will probably only get a small number of these until he builds up a reputation and can be recommended.

In order to get leads for the major installation work he will have to also offer emergency repair work.

The tendering for jobs will mean visiting clients in the evenings and at weekends.

Emergency repairs will mean being on call 24 hours a day.

His strong desire to be deliver excellent customer service at all times is just not compatible with emergency call outs or tendering for work.

He investigates the possibility of sub-contracting to building firms. This would mean he would not have to tender for work during unsociable hours or carry out emergency repairs. The down side would be that there would be periods of very long hours to meet deadlines, prolonged delays due to bad weather and the possibility of having to travel further afield to secure continuous work.

Joe has been looking at the growing market of people renting accommodation rather than buying. This has led to a whole new generation of buy-to-let landlords.

These buy-to-let landlords have to make sure that the properties that they let are safe and one of the stipulations is that central heating systems have an annual safety inspection by a qualified inspector.

Often these buy-to-let landlords will use the service of letting agents to manage properties for them. Joe decides to contact the letting agents, where his customer service skills can be put to good use and then use his technical capabilities to manage the central heating safety aspects for the letting agents.

If he is successful at this he will not have to tender for work, he will not be obliged to carry out emergency repairs and he will be in a position where there is annual repeat business due to the compulsory nature of the inspections.

The safety inspections will help Joe to develop great relationships with letting agents, who will continually find him new clients, and he can decide what other services to offer or sub-contract out. If Joe decides to expand his business he can employ other qualified inspectors on a fixed fee per inspection, this would do away with the variable and complex nature of something like bathroom installations.

If you meet Joe and he tells you he is a Plumber you would be forgiven for imaging him with a wrench in his hand fixing a leaking tap.

Joe never gets called out to emergencies, he never works weekends, he never tenders for a job and he will never be out of work.

Joe took the time to understand what the impact could be if he created a business in the most obvious way, in the image of someone else.

As you decide how your business will operate are you clear about the implications your decisions may have and have you, like Joe, explored other alternatives.

You are the King; once you've chosen a Kingdom how you reign is up to you.

Chapter 3

Step 3: Getting you prepared for your new business life. Things will "feel" different and you will have new challenges and decisions that you haven't faced before. This is your future, come and take a look.

Chapter 3.0 – If you don't ask...

When you are starting out you are ideally placed to get feedback and advice from people. Normally all you have to do is ask.

You could contact a local Business Big Wig and see if they would see you for an hour, you will be surprised at how many will say yes.

People like to talk, and everyone's favourite subject is themselves.

What you need to do is work out what questions you really want an answer to.

Whilst people will talk there is a problem that we are all not used to really thinking about what we are saying and therefore the advice you will get will probably fall short of what it could be.

Try asking a friend about a recent holiday they went on. Ask them why they chose the particular Country/resort. See what response you get. Don't let them off the hook, keep delving until you uncover something about their decision, after all they could have potentially gone anywhere in the world.

Get used to asking questions, the best questions are always "Why"; pretend that you are 2 years old again. People find these questions difficult to answer; they have to put more effort in and if you let them talk and you actively listen you will be pleasantly surprised at what you will find out.

There are numerous technical experts in your chosen field and industry who will gladly share information with you if you ask the right questions.

The next time you have a meeting with a potential supplier, who wants to talk about price, service levels, and range etc. try to think of the conversation and your goals in a different way.

Yes, you want to find out about what they offer, however, what you really want is information and knowledge that you don't possess but this person sat opposite you or is on the phone with you just might.

What are the latest trends? Who is their biggest customer? How have they grown their business? If they were in your shoes what would they being differently?

Most sales people that I have met are normally highly motivated to close a sale and therefore more than willing to help you.

You must understand that **the person opposite is willing to share their experience, skills and knowledge with you if you would only ask the right questions**. How much is this worth to you?

You can be more forthright if you want to and ask a question like "Could you give me 5 examples on how your service/company can help me grow my business?"

Then sit back and listen. I did this once with a Sales Person and the next day his Managing Director called me and offered to develop a website for me and provide a few thousand brochures, all for free, on top of the prices and service levels they had offered.

Remember, that as a King you are the ultimate decision maker in your business, people love dealing with decision makers.

This book is interactive. To access more content for free please visit www.**sufian.me/keepcalm**

Chapter 3.1 – Communication let me down

Without exception everywhere you have ever worked has had communication problems.

I will just deal with verbal communication, rather than no-verbal or written, to illustrate a key area in your potential success.

My view of the root cause of a communication problem is that as human beings we can virtually all speak and as a consequence we all believe that we can do it well.

I define communication as "**the passing and understanding of information between two or more people**".

This is the first step.

The second step is checking understanding, if you ever carry out any training you will often come across the "nod of ignorance". Explain something and then look at the whites of people's eyes and ask them whether they understand. They will generally nod. An experienced trainer and communicator will check for understanding.

"Eddie you understand that 2 squared is 4 (nod of ignorance in response) could you please tell me what 3 squared is. "6" comes the reply. Eddie has been adding the numbers rather than multiplying.

So always check understanding.

The final step is context.

It is Friday afternoon, a little after 1pm, Geoff the Sales Director, asks Debbie the Office Manager to be look out for an important call from a new client at around 3pm.

It is a busy office and at around 3pm Debbie has let a couple of the staff go for a short break, suddenly 3 lines light up and Debbie answers.

The following Monday all hell is breaking lose. The Managing Director has Geoff in to explain why they haven't secured this order that was going to save the business. Geoff blames Debbie as he "told her to expect the phone call at 3pm last Friday" and she failed to answer the call, the potential client saw this as a sign of things to come and pulled out of the deal.

The reality is that the fault lies with Geoff; he should have made it crystal clear to Debbie how important the phone call was. If she was distracted when he was speaking to her he should have dealt with this.

"Debbie I need your undivided attention, so please stop what you are doing and listen to me".

He could then have explained in detail that if there was only one phone call answered that afternoon it should be that one. Debbie would not have let anyone leave the office for any reason and indeed might have drafted others into the office just to be confident that the call would be dealt with. She wasn't given the option.

As the leader of your business you set the standard for communication and you are left with the consequences of poor communication and the benefits of great communication.

Every CV (resume) I have ever read states that the person can communicate effectively at all levels within an organisation, really?

Work at being crystal clear with your communication, check understanding and above all provide context for important events. It will be very rare for anyone to have their normal pattern interrupted for someone to say something important to them. They will remember.

You are the King; communicated clearly at all times.

Chapter 3.2 – Hunting we will go

People generally don't like sales because they feel as though they are being hunted, and if you are trying to sell you are the Hunter which can be even more uncomfortable.

If you are hung up about sales then you really need to get over it. We will cover the new reality of sales in a later chapter but for now let's deal with your mind set and perspective.

Do you believe that you have a great product/service?

Do you believe that your product will make a positive difference to people?

Are you proud to stand behind your product and service and declare that this is who you are and what you do?

Are you aware of competitors and products that are not as good as yours?

Do you not have a responsibility to let all potential customers make a choice and have the opportunity to buy your products and services?

Would you be doing potential customers a disservice by not letting them know about your products/ services?

If you answered yes to all these questions then this is your reason and motivation to market and sell your products.

You understand that to achieve this you will encounter some people who will not want your products, this is inevitable, but should not detract you from trying to reach the ones that do.

People can always switch off, opt out and keep their money in their pockets, that's their prerogative.

You are the King; be proud of what you stand for.

Chapter 3.3 – Pass me the rule book

You are the King. You set the rules.

You can take inspiration from looking at how other businesses operate; indeed if you buy a franchise you will be given the rules in the form of a written down "operations manual".

The truth is, other than the obvious legal requirements, there are no rules.

You have a complete blank sheet to create the world that is your business.

This is both liberating and frightening in equal measure. You will no doubt find yourself gravitating to a particular way of doing things, this is natural.

Don't operate on auto pilot; start out as you mean to go on.

Think about all the good things that you liked about where you used to work, or the great things you see in companies that you admire and emulate them where appropriate and ditch the things you hated.

I used to hate meetings, by any account I achieved Mastery years ago. Now if I do have meetings, sometimes there is just no avoiding them, they are meaningful with clear objectives and do not last very long.

You are the King; this is your Kingdom.

Chapter 3.4 – Poets, Priest & Politicians

In forming the rules and parameters for your new Kingdom you will seek out advisors. Sometimes these will be professionals such as Accountants, Bank Managers, Solicitors and sometimes they will be just people that you respect.

If you have never had to deal directly with a Professional and been responsible for paying their fees this can be quite a daunting experience. Suddenly you are this tiny business visiting grand premises of firms that have been there for decades if not centuries. They are professionals; they know what they are doing. They are there to advise you and you would be a fool not to listen.

At the end of the day these professionals will not be providing you directly with clients, they will not be paying your suppliers or dealing with any staff issues that may arise.

One of the roles of professionals is to offer advice based upon their knowledge and experience, again if this relates to legal requirements and technicalities then please take notice and act. The vast majority of the time the discussions will not be about legal compliance but rather about general business issues and opportunities.

Given that you are used to listening to these professionals and taking their advice on compliance issues, you trust them and probably like them too, it is very easy to fall into the trap of taking all their advice.

Remember, you are the King; you seek out advice from the people around you that are best placed to provide the advice and input you require, however, the final decision is yours, it will always be yours.

If you are always using someone else's judgement then who really is running the company and if the advisor is not around what will be the consequences.

You should always be in a position where you have a fuller picture than anyone else about your business and therefore you can interpret advice like no one else.

You are the King; select your advisors wisely and listen.

Chapter 3.5 – Time to abdicate

You are great at delegating, skills that you picked up on your journey through the corporate world. If you are not great at delegating then you are really going to struggle.

The trouble with delegating when you are the King is that this can sometimes fall into the realms of abdication when you are running your own business.

Most businesses when they first start outsource part of what they do, this is invariably finance/accounts, and as such I will use this as an example but it could be any function of your business.

You need to provide various transactional details, sales invoices, purchase invoices etc. From all the data you provide an Accountant or Book Keeper will put these into a standardised format that will meet legal requirements and produce Balance Sheets, Profit & Loss Accounts, Management Accounts, Cash Flow Forecasts etc.

This information is vital to tell you how you are doing financially, what plans you need to put in place, how much tax you will paying, whether you need to borrow any funds etc.

Once you trust someone and have delegated responsibility to them it is all too easy to assume that they are doing a great job and that everything is fine.

Remember that at the end of the day you are responsible for your business. If you file Accounts each year and these are prepared by qualified Chartered Accountants they will still require your signature as owner/director saying that these accounts are a true picture of your trading position and that the information is accurate.

The first time I signed such Accounts I asked a question about this as I had virtually no idea how the Accounts had arrived in the format that was presented to me and was signing purely on trust. The other thing to note was the Accountants were not being held responsible for the accuracy of the data, I was. I signed and smiled wryly.

I grew the business and had my own administration department and people responsible for the preparation of the financial information which was overseen by my Accountants. I made a BIG MISTAKE that I do not want you to copy. I abdicated responsibility for this area of the business because I was so focused on other issues.

I failed to manage the delegation, I went missing and all was not as well as it might have been. I should have been more involved and demanded key performance information to be explained to me every week, I didn't.

If you met a friend and decided to visit a shopping mall and your friend starting buying lots of expensive new clothes you would pay attention and make comments. If on the other hand you had agreed to pay for the clothes that your friend was trying on how differently would you feel and react? At what point would you put a limit on the spending and alter your friend's behaviour.

You are a King, delegate but never abdicate.

Chapter 3.6 - Now take away the safety net

The single biggest barrier to starting a business is procrastination. A million reasons why not to do something. This can be linked to the desire to be perfect.

What are the most productive days of your year normally?

They are the last days at work before your vacation/holiday, why?

These days are self-imposed deadlines. Deadlines are wonderful for ways of getting action and avoiding inertia.

The next time you see a banner on a shop that tells you when it is about to re-open whilst it is closed for refurbishment imagine this. Someone has set a deadline and numerous contractors are all trying to meet the deadline. Invariably the deadline will be met, however if you were to visit the shop the day before or even a few hours before the opening you would see a whirl wind of activity and probably chaos.

At the end of the day at the appointed time the shop re-opens, not everything is perfect, but the shop is ready to greet customers again.

The deadline could have been a week or 8 weeks, it doesn't really matter, the fact that it is a deadline on the horizon is enough.

Deadlines are your friend, deadlines focus everyone to a single goal, and deadlines are simple, deadlines equal action.

The second thing that happens on the days before you go on holiday is that you become super-efficient, your brain goes into hyper drive and you don't let anything distract you. Your safety net of extra time has gone. Without this safety net you are forced to act, and boy how you respond, you do a week's work in a day.

Start this great habit today, imagine you are going on holiday, set yourself a deadline for reading this book and stick to it. Set yourself a deadline for starting your business.

On the last day at work before you go on holiday what are the time consuming things that you automatically avoid, what are the distraction magnates that add no value to your life?

Your goal is not to become someone else it is to become the best that you can be, to give you the best possibility of achieving your goals and dreams. Remember it is not *who* you are that is going to make a difference it is *what* you do that matters.

You are the King and what you do defines you.

> This book is interactive. To access more content for free please visit www.sufian.me/keepcalm

Chapter 3.7 - And now for my next trick

Taking action is a very important step. Completing something and having perseverance is equally as important.

The desire for perfection, the fear of failure and the comfort of the familiar are all contributors to never completing a task.

We have mentioned perfection before in business, it doesn't exist, know when to stop and identify when enough is enough.

The fear of failure is common to everyone. Even in your high powered corporate world there was **always the fear that someone was going to "find you out", that you were a charlatan**. We all have this fear; it's natural and should not stop you from completing your task and showing it to the world.

The worst that can happen is that you get negative feedback. This is great as it provides invaluable information for you to act upon.

The comfort of the familiar is the most difficult thing to address. This means change, this means being out of your comfort zone. The fact is that you will have to face up to this. Try to meet this challenge as an opportunity to discover more about yourself.

Recently I was watching a documentary about a programme on the BBC called The Great British Bake Off. The format is quite simple and has been a huge success in the UK with prime TV audiences in the millions, making it one of the most watched programmes in the country.

A group of amateur bakers are set challenges each week to bake something for a couple of experts; all the activity takes place in a large marquee. The programme runs for a number of weeks and the baker's efforts are critiqued and marked by the experts with an elimination each week until eventually we are left with a winner.

It has entered the psyche of the British public and encouraged people to re-engage with their love of baking or discover baking for the very first time.
What is of real interest is the "journey" of some of the contestants. The

programme followed up these enthusiastic amateur bakers a year after the series had finished.

Remember that these people had a particular skill and interest in baking; they were from a diverse range of backgrounds, ethnicities and ages.

What was amazing and heart-warming was the high number of these finalists, as they competed with thousands of other entrants to get to the televised show, who had now discovered a complete change of direction in their lives.

Some were making a living as public speakers who were entertaining people with their baking prowess in front of a live paying audience, others had been offered their own TV Shows, others were using their celebrity to educate people and some were starting businesses based around their passion.

They all described how this was the best experience of their lives. How did this happen? Why hadn't this happened to them before?

Some of them had careers that you would class as vocations, such as teaching, before they decided to dedicate themselves to baking after appearing on this television reality show.

Some of the more cynical of you would ask to re-visit these people in 5 years' time to see how the land lies and then you would be able to make a judgement. That is not the point. The point is that these people firstly took action, they did not procrastinate. Secondly they showed tenacity, resilience and dedication to compete week after week and most importantly they then did something special with this opportunity. They assessed their lives, they decided to take a risk, they decided to try something new, and they decided to make themselves feel uncomfortable.

Will it work out wonderfully as they would like for each and every one of them, probably not.

They will, whatever the outcome, have found out more about themselves than they could ever have imagined. They will have realised that they have the power to do anything when they put their minds to it. They will have learnt that getting out there and doing stuff is what makes a difference.

You are a King, take a lesson from the bakers, switch the oven on and make something special.

Chapter 3.8 - Why did you start a business?

I get asked this question frequently. Sometimes it is worded differently, "did you always know that you were entrepreneurial?"

The truth is I didn't know. I didn't identify this element of my personality until I already had a business. When I worked in the corporate world I would always work as though every decision had an immediate and real impact on the shareholders.

As I climbed the career ladder I realised that I wanted to take risks that others were not willing to take. I despised the politics that took place and I was absolutely useless at it, I tried it once and I can still feel the taste in my mouth now. I always tried to be true to myself and this was both a benefit and a major failing when you are working for someone else.

I felt compelled to start my own business and struggled for years contemplating what this would be, I was focused on the wrong question.

When I started my business I still looked upon myself as a Professional Manager. That is what I did, that is what I had always done. It wasn't until I met someone one day, someone with much more experience than me, who described me as an Entrepreneur.

I was shocked and intrigued; this guy had only just met me for 5 minutes. He went on to prove to me that I was an entrepreneur. "Do you hate admin?" he asked me. "Yes" I replied.

"Are you inconsistent with managing your staff?" Once again I replied "Yes".

"Are you always looking to create the next thing and eager to get onto the next project?" "Yes" I replied.

"You are an Entrepreneur" he said. "You may be good, even great as a Manager, but you are an Entrepreneur and probably a serial one".

Sometimes people observing you can see things that you cannot. From that day on, after much thought, I decided that I was an Entrepreneur. This is how I was going to see myself and it made me feel comfortable. I still see myself the same way today, many years later. I am thankful for the observation that helped to free me even more.

This might not be you now or ever. Your job is to find out exactly what makes you tick. It is a never ending journey, just like the people on the Great British Bake Off, some of whom it might have taken over 60 years to articulate and take the plunge.

You are a King; make sure you are a King of your own making and in your own image.

Chapter 3.9 – Marketing Plumbers

Almost without exception you will be confronted with Marketing Plumbers when you start your business. You might not meet them in person; they might be on the internet, via recommendation or you came across them just by chance.

They feed and exist on your deep seated fear that you are missing out on something and that if you don't act now you will be left behind.

Marketing Plumbers are people who will convince you that you really need to spend some money carrying out a particular form of advertising (they might well call this Marketing – I will explain what Marketing really is for a small business in later chapters).

Marketing Plumbers have always existed; however, with the growth of technology and new ways of interacting with potential customers they are now nearing epidemic proportions.

If we went back 20 years the options open for a small business to try and reach a potential audience were quite limited. You had a choice of local newspapers, local radio, flyers delivered to households, trade fayres, direct mail, cold calling prospects and magazines such as Yellow Pages.

If I was going to persuade you to spend money on advertising and I worked for a magazine directory like, Yellow Pages, I would probably try this route.

I would show you a copy of last year's addition, show you various areas that I thought that you should advertise in and then focus in on a competitor. The magazine is geographically based and there is quite a high chance that you will be aware of the competitors, especially the largest ones with largest advertising budgets.

I would explain that the biggest players, who have been around for many years, are taking full page listings. They know that this works and continue to advertise year on year.

I would tell you what the circulation of the magazine is and describe how in one month your advert would be delivered to 500,000 houses and businesses.

That would be my proof; I have convinced you of the value. I haven't sold directly to you because I have had the competition do that for me. The only question left is to see what size of listing would be appropriate and whether you could cope with all the work that this would bring in.

By now you should be able to see straight thru me and be able to focus in on the things that matter to you. If you can't see straight thru me then let me help you to understand.

What information are we assuming based upon the information I have presented?

Firstly, we are assuming that the people already advertising in the magazine have made the correct financial decision by advertising and that the pay back on their investment far out ways the outlay. Why else would they continue to advertise year after year?

The fact of the matter is that these people do not carry out return on investment calculations (ROI) on this advertising spend. Secondly, when customers purchase from them they do not ask or record where the lead came from.

Secondly, we fixate on the 500,000 circulation numbers and relate this to the price. The reality is that a very small percentage of the circulation actually purchases what you sell in any given year; let's say 1%, so this leaves us with the potential to get our business in front of 5,000 and not 500,000.

When we look at how people use the magazine we find that 80% of people are using this to look up the contact details of a business they already know, and this is not you. Now the potential market is 1,000.

Of the remaining 1,000, who might want to find a new provider or are first time buyers, only 500 of this use the magazine as they are given contacts from personal recommendations. Of the 500 who use the magazine 80% go for the largest adverts, which leave a potential of 100 who will look up your details. Of these 20 % will become customers.

We started out with 500,000 prospects and we are left with 20. Now if each sale is worth £1million pounds this still might be a great investment, the reality is that the sale and more importantly the profit from the sale or the Gross Profit, will probably not get anywhere near the investment.

The reason why I call these people Marketing Plumbers is because they do not understand your business, they do not understand what you are trying to achieve, they do not understand who your customers are and what messages are going to resonate with them, instead they offer a solution without understanding anything.

Let me use a bricks and mortar analogy to illustrate.

Your business is a plot of land. You haven't yet decided what you want to build on this land. You have chosen a location and the land is level.

Someone knocks on your door and offers you a thousand red roof tiles at a great discount. The guy peddling these is the Marketing Plumber. He tells you what great quality these tiles are and that they will last a life time. They are genuinely a great deal. You consider whether to purchase them or not.

The reason you are considering whether to purchase them or not is because you do not yet know enough about your business and your potential customers. When you have planned and made your decision you will instantly either reject the Marketing Plumber and not even let him start a conversation with you. "No thanks, I don't need to listen to what you are offering" you will say or you will listen and decide whether the offer is just too great an opportunity to turn down.

To be able to say "no" is a wonderful and liberating thing. Saying "yes" or "maybe" is easy. Saying "no" means that you understand exactly what you want and where you are going.

You have decided that on this land of yours you are going to build a tennis court, a grass tennis court no less (with no roof!).

When the Marketing Plumber tries to offer you the red roof tiles you don't even let him speak, you know that you do not need them now or in the future, they are not part of your plans.

The examples with the magazine and the land are easy to digest; however, today the Marketing Plumbers are everywhere. Someone invents the latest Social Media application and the Marketing Plumbers will breed and tell you that you simply must be on this new platform. They will tell you the story of someone they know, or who they have heard of, who has had great success using it. Be prepared, be able to spot a Marketing Plumber and move on.

I am emphasising this area because it is a very dangerous area and could potentially destroy your business. **It could destroy your business by haemorrhaging cash or by taking up enormous amounts of time trying to learn a new and useless skill.**

It could also make you worry needlessly about something that shouldn't be cluttering your brain.

You are the King; understand your people and what they want before accepting offers of help by misguided opportunists.

This book is interactive. To access more content for free please visit www.**sufian.me/keepcalm**

Chapter 3.10 – The Joy of Networking

Let's imagine that it is the first day of the rest of your life and you have started your very own business.

After having years of a full diary and various meetings to attend and deadlines to meet you are now free.

You stare at the blank pages of a diary; the phone is not ringing, your email box is empty. You get the picture.

Someone suggests that you need to get out there and get involved with the local business community. Sounds like a great idea and you have the time. You are filled with excitement and enthusiasm and this will be an opportunity to meet like-minded people and maybe get a sale, who knows?

I use the term like-minded as I really cannot think of a better description, what I mean by it is people who share your values, want the same goals as you and who you would feel comfortable in the company of.

Networking events are gatherings of business people who in theory are like-minded. They come in differing formats and they either have one or both of the following goals.

Firstly, they are there to promote your business. To find other business owners who will recommend you to their contacts and you in return will reciprocate. You've spotted a flaw. You don't have any customers yet. You may need suppliers though and this might be a great place to get recommendations on suppliers or meet them in person.

Secondly, they are they as a social group. Running your own business can be very lonely and these days it is possible to run a business with your eyes glued to a computer screen and never see another living soul for days on end.

You research the local area and you find out there are lots of networking events taking places, every week and almost every day.

Most of the events take place first thing in the morning so that it doesn't interfere with the normal working day.

You will see events that advertise as "free". What does this mean?

This means that there is no attendance fee, a small payment normally to cover the cost of a coffee or a small breakfast roll.

There is no such thing as a free lunch. You will have heard this many times. This is true and this is why it is true.

The one commodity that we all share and that cannot be bought, traded or refunded is time. When you run your own business, especially when you are the business in the early days means that decisions on how, where and what you do with your time are critical.

If you were not doing X what else could you be concentrating on? Your time is not free, it is a very scarce resource, use it wisely.

Other Networking Groups will let you attend an event as a guest and then there will normally be an annual subscription fee to pay. Some Groups will generate a sense of scarcity by only allowing one company to be represented for a particular service, such as one Graphic Designer, whilst others will happily accept any number of Graphic Designers.

Now we have added real financial cost and time.

If you ask a Networking Group member how much time they commit to the Networking Group each week they will tell how the meetings last for, these will typical be around 90 minutes.

They will not tell you how long the travelling takes, how they have re-arranged their schedules to attend and how much time they have spent thinking about how they might be able to help other members of the Group. Some Groups will have an attendance policy, meaning that if you miss, let's say, 2 meetings in a year and do not arrange for a substitute to take your place you will lose your membership of the group and your subscription fee.

You will be told that the Group only want a person who is committed to helping each other and that is why they have these rules in place. You will be convinced by the argument that if you are to commit yourself, is it not unreasonable to expect that others will have made a strong commitment to you as well?

The people that are members will be evangelical in their support for the Group and the organisation, they will tell you that they were just like you when they started out and describe how much value they have received from being members.

It is not my job to persuade you one way or another as to whether attending a Networking event, and which types of these, is the right thing to do for you and your business. My goal is for you to have the tools and sometimes knowledge at your disposal to make the correct decision for you.

You know who your target market is; you should have developed a marketing plan on how you want to reach these potential customers. If you haven't, don't worry, I will cover this later in the book.

Let me give you some more information and perspective on Networking. I am doing this because a lot of people enter into organised Networking as it is very seductive. One of the reasons it is seductive is that you believe that it is not selling, that customers will be brought to you by the existing businesses. If this was true how great would it be? It would be great because almost everyone wants to avoid selling.

You probably didn't start your business because you loved selling, in the back of your mind you know that selling will be involved but at this moment in time you equate selling with pain. We will cover this later in the book.

It is time to take a closer look at the people who organise the Networking events. Some of the organisers are volunteers whilst others are running this as a commercial venture. You can find this out if you want to.

The thing that they have in common is that they have made a decision to commit to the Group you are looking to join. They had choices and decisions to make and this is the one that they made.

Any decision that requires commitment, and reinforces our self-image especially when we are asked to publicly declare this, results in a strong case of confirmation bias kicking in.

A confirmation bias is a tendency for people to favour information that confirms their preconceptions or hypotheses regardless of whether the information is true.

A simple example of this is that if you believe that all hoody wearing teenagers are hell bent on causing social unrest and carry out the majority of crime in society you will actively seek out articles, media, friends etc. that will reinforce this view. You will ignore information that challenges and is contrary to your preconceived notions.

Whenever your opinions or beliefs are intertwined with your self-image you couldn't pull them away without damaging your concept of your self, you avoid situationa which may cause harm to those beliefs.
So the Netwroking Group organisers can become so confident in their view of the world that no one could possibly change their mind.
If we look at the facts, when someone joins a Networking Group the average length of membership, in the UK, is around 18 months.

Does this mean that after 18 months the Networking has been so effective that there is no further need to attend or does it mean that the Networking didn't work out?

Each year there are hundreds of thousands of people like you starting a business, a steady stream of inexperienced people with hopes and dreams and want to believe that Networking will deliver what the organisers say that it will.

If you pay for something you are more likely to commit. If you pay up front for something then you are even more likely to commit, you would feel robbed if you didn't get your money's worth.

In paying for a year in advance you are making a public statement that you will commit for a year. Your self-image and core values are now at stake.

Ask yourself why you are doing this? What do you want to get out of it? What does success look like? What is the real cost, in time and money?

I attended events like this over a decade ago. I worked out that I was spending 200 hours per year networking in one Group. This was the equivalent to 5 weeks solid work a year. In fuel, subscription fees and breakfasts it was costing around £3000 per year. The extra business we received was nil. The reason I joined was to grow the business network not to get any moral support and to socialise. After a few months I sent one of my Managers, after a few months he asked whether he could stop going and then we sent another Manager as part of her development. We didn't renew for the second year, so we were slightly lower in attendance than the 18 month average.

Now let's take a look at the people attending the events.

If you asked a hundred people at a Networking event to raise their hands if they were here to sell, guess what, a hundred hands would be in the air. Now ask the same people to raise their hands if they are here to buy and there will be no hands raised.

If you are there to sell you are in for a disappointment. A Networking event is there to make connections, to start new mutually beneficial relationships.

There are various different types of people that you will come across at networking events; here I will cover just a couple. You have been warned.

The first is the fledgling Entrepreneur. He is awkward socially but forthright. He is out of his comfort zone. He has been advised to "get out there" and "meet people".

In a crowded room of people with name tags he will march straight up to you. He will introduce himself, even if you are already in mid conversation with someone else, thrust his business card at you and ask whether you have one.

You will be polite and take his card and give him yours. He will not look at your card. You will look at his. He will then proceed to tell everything about his business and try to sell to you; a Networking mugging.

You will listen politely and internally scream "please go away". When he has finished you will smile, you won't have the motivation to respond. You will wish him well and then watch him accost someone else.

I feel so sorry for this guy. He is trying his best to do what he has been told is the right thing to do. He is way outside of his comfort zone and yet it is all wasted energy. He could in fact be doing his business a great deal of harm.

The second type I will look at now is the Networking Professional. There are at least 2 types of these I will describe the most ubiquitous one of these.

They are much more sophisticated than the fledgling. They will be dressed for business, very smartly turned out. They will introduce themselves to you and ask you about your business. They will ask you specific questions such as "Who is your ideal customer?", "If I could introduce you to one person or company who what that be and why?"

You will talk and your lack of ability to directly answer their questions will leave you feeling as though you have just met someone who really gets networking, is good at it (at least much better than you) and would be a great contact to develop.

Even if you have just started you own business and feel that you don't know anyone, you actually do. You still have friends, previous colleagues, family etc. and the person you have just met has a product that could benefit any number of these contacts.

Your product/service by its very nature is for a very narrow niche market and therefore you don't feel it is really possible that you could meet someone who would have specific contacts that would help you grow your sales quickly.

If you decide to attend networking events have a clear objective in mind. If you meet people for 5 minutes over a coffee and swap business cards then you must must must follow it up.

Networking events are a little bit like meetings. At the time they can be very enjoyable, some of the guest speakers are entertaining but a few days afterwards you cannot remember a great deal about them.

You are the King; promise yourself that if you do attend networking events it will be because it makes sense to you or simply because you just want to.

Chapter 3.11 - The Company you keep

You are about to enter the World of Business. There are many people out there who have skills that you do not possess, who have experience that you do not have and a perspective and insight that you may never achieve.

Find more intelligent and more successful people than you and connect with them.

If you have any "energy vampires", "mood hoovers" or whatever else you want to call them that are bringing you down, stay away from them if you can. This is difficult if they are family. If they are family then don't discuss your business with them, don't try and convince them of anything, this is taking away energy that you need to be able to focus on the real things that matter.

An "energy vampire" is someone who leaves you feeling drained with their negativity; you must know someone like this.

When you make a connection with someone who can help you grow you are in effect borrowing some of their life experiences, attitudes and knowledge that you do not have. This could be invaluable to you.

Similarly people will want to engage with you because you are enthusiastic and have a can do attitude. They will also benefit from being around you in other ways, it is a reciprocal relationship.

There is normally a reason why successful people are successful, remember that what you are embarking on is really difficult for any one person to achieve. It is not a sign of weakness to seek help or advice on the contrary it is an intelligent sign of strength and eagerness to achieve your goals.

If you don't have the opportunity to access these people, for whatever reason, and then become of a student of teachers that you admire and avoid becoming a fan. There are millions of teachers to be found on the Internet.

You are the King; surround yourself with the best people and invest your time and money wisely.

Chapter 4
Step 4: Businesses are about people. It is now time to take a look at employees from a different perspective.

Chapter 4.0 – The truth about staff

This could and probably should be an entire book in its own right.

If you have made the decision that you need to directly employ someone or many people then please read this section carefully.

If you are not planning on ever directly employing anyone as your business model doesn't require this then have a read anyway as this will only make you feel even better than you do right now and will also help if your circumstances alter.

In every survey you will ever see about how employees feel about their Managers you will find that they comment on how ineffective they are and how dissatisfied they are with them in general.

No great surprises there right. You want to think that as a Manager you were much better than an average Manager, that you cared and you were effective. We'll park this bus for a moment.

Think about everywhere you have ever worked and think about people that you have worked with or are working with. Again I have to remind you that I am in the UK.

If you were paying their wages out of your own pocket how many of these colleagues you would you quite happily pay? This would be based on what you think or know they are currently getting paid to do a job working for you based on the following criteria.

- They have mastery of their chosen field or position.

- They are highly motivated and love their job and it shows in their 100% commitment.

- They are great team players.

- They understand and are committed to the goals of the company.

- You believe that they are 100% worth the wages and benefits that they receive.

How are you doing? Have you thought of anyone yet?

Take your time, this is your money.

Maybe you are thinking that some of your colleagues would be better in an environment created by you and that this would alter and improve how they perform?

Now think about the people that you come into contact with on a day to day basis, at the Supermarket, at the coffee shop and other establishments where great people skills would be a major advantage.

Think about friends that you have, how do they feel about their job? How many of them are looking to move jobs or are disgruntled and always complaining about their Manager or just about their pay or some other work related issues?

Now when you are an observer it is interesting to stand back and take a different perspective. Think about it, you are probably realising that the vast majority of people that you know or come into contact with probably shouldn't be in that job, if they have the skills for that job they are probably looking for another job or dissatisfied in some other way.

It is quite sad to contemplate, people who feel restricted and trapped because they do not see that they have any viable other options at the moment.

How many of these people chose to be doing the role that they currently have? Or did the job choose them out of necessity or just plain convenience?

How many times have you seen a survey from Managers about the people that they are responsible for?

The truth is this:

- most people are in the wrong job
- most people never "master" the job they are in
- most people are inherently lazy and will avoid work when they can
- most people are not loyal to their employer, they are loyal to themselves and their family

You are probably thinking that I am wrong; am I right? Before I started my own business I would have agreed with you.

You are probably thinking that if people are in the wrong job this is down to poor recruitment and selection. This is not a mistake that you will make. We will come back to this in the section on recruitment.

You are probably thinking that people can "master" a job, if that is what is required, given the right environment, the correct recruitment and the appropriate training.

You are probably thinking that if you recruit the right people and motivate and remunerate them appropriately that you will avoid the inherent laziness of the masses.

Finally, you are probably thinking that people are not loyal to large corporations where everyone is a number, a slave; however your organisation, your small organisation, will be caring, it will be like a family and people will be loyal and they will care.

Let me tell you what experienced business owners have to say. They won't say it in public because they would upset their employees and be cast outside of society as being repulsive and evil.

The single word that experience business owners use about their staff is "nightmare".

I have spoken to hundreds of experienced business owners at length about this topic and there is a general consensus here that is only spoken of in a safe environment of like-minded business owners.

Normally the realisation that staff is a "nightmare", I will elaborate on this, takes years to materialise.

In the first years of your first business you normally don't accept what some people have said about staff, you have just come out of the corporate world and you will make a difference. You are better than them.

It also takes a few years to have the experience. This is often the difference between intellectually being to understand something and really living, feeling and knowing something in your very core. If you have children you will have experienced this.

Why do people say that employees are a "nightmare"?

Everything I have already mentioned comes together and manifests itself in the following ways.

There will be no one who cares about your business as much as you. You might convince yourself otherwise, but this is simply not the case. The stakes for you are high. This is your dream, this is your Kingdom. Everyone else will tell you what you want to hear, at the end of the day you pay their wages.

Caring Jenny

This is the story of Jenny. She employed around 20 people at any given time and around a dozen of these had been with her for over 10 years, when she first started the business.

They were her friends, they were a family. Hard times hit and they rallied together, everyone pitched in.

Things got worse and some months Jenny barely had enough money to pay the wages, she took on debts to make sure everyone got paid. The only person who did not get paid was Jenny.

She should have let some members of staff go, but she knew that they had children to support so she kept them on, even though the business couldn't afford it. The staff in return agreed to have a pay freeze.

The business failed and went into administration. Some of her key staff had found positions immediately with a competitor; they even got the job of buying some of Jenny's assets from the administrator.

Other staff took cases against Jenny to recover money's they had been told they would be entitled to, even though they knew Jenny had done everything that she could to keep them employed when she could have let them go.

Jenny started hearing how some of the staff used to steal from her and were selling products behind her back. It was all too much. The money was hard enough to swallow; it was the trust and disloyalty that hurt the most.

I met Jenny a couple of years after this had happened and she was just about able to recount her story without crying. She is tough, she has been taught a lesson that will live with her forever.

Everyone will think that as a business owner you are doing better financially than you are and are therefore fair game.

Pragmatic Liam

Before I started my first business a guy called Liam told me this cautionary story. He started by telling me that it probably wouldn't make a difference to me and my approach to managing people, but he was going to tell me anyway.

Every Xmas Liam would organise a Xmas do for his staff. He wouldn't allow partners to come; he would have free food and a free bar. The evening would be organised so that the staff did not have to work the following day.

"Imagine", said Liam, "if at the Xmas party I gathered all the staff around and thanked them for their efforts during the year and handed them each a brown envelope with cash inside. The money had already been put through the payroll and all appropriate taxes paid."

The envelopes had £10,000 bonus in for each of the staff, in cash.

"After thanking me", said Liam, "the first thought that they would have is, I wonder how much money Liam has made?"

To illustrate his point Liam continued by moving forward to the Xmas party the following year. Everything was the same; the business had done very well again.

This year after he thanked them Liam again handed out the brown envelopes, this year they had £9,000 pounds inside each of them.

"What do you think their reaction would be?" Liam asked. "I'll tell you, he continued, they would be annoyed, they would be disappointed and they would think that I was exploiting them and still making a fortune."

"So, I don't play those games. I don't care what my staff thinks of me, and I rarely think of them. We have a contract in place, an employment contract. I stick to my side of it and provide work, a safe environment and the agreed remuneration. Their side of the contract is to provide their labour, skills and knowledge."

He looked at me. I must have looked shocked and astonished and a little bit of true disbelief at the callousness of this man.

Liam smiled; "I told you that you probably wouldn't listen. Come back and see me in 10 years' time".

Disappointed Estate Agents

Another story was told to me by two partners, Debbie and Mark, who ran an Estate Agency, with around 10 retail branches all in one city.

They had grown the company quickly. The business revolved around customer service and sales. A main area to be able to make increased profits was in financial services.

Someone buys a house; they might need a mortgage or life assurance. Each branch had a financial advisor.

Debbie and Mark decided to visit every branch and announce that they were going to have a competition for the next quarter, leading up to the summer. The competition was based upon each branches performance on referring clients to the financial advisors. They were each set a minimum target to reach to qualify for the competition and then the winner would be selected from the qualifiers based upon actual achieved sales and number of referrals.

The prize was a trip to New York, all expenses paid, for 3 nights and £1000 spending money.

As you can image the staff were very excited and so were Debbie and Mark. For the next 3 months every time Debbie or Mark visited a branch the New York Competition was on everyone's lips.

Unfortunately for Debbie and Mark the enthusiasm didn't convert itself into action or results. At the end of the deadline no single branch had even reached their qualification target. This didn't stop the discussions or expectations at branch level.

I'll let Debbie explain. "Every time we visited a branch all the staff wanted to talk about was the competition, who had won, why hadn't we announced the winner yet. We explained that no one achieved their targets. It did no good. Eventually after weeks of this, Mark got out his credit card at one of our monthly Manager's meetings and asked the Managers to draw lots for the prize."

"At the end of the day we wanted to do something good, we wanted to reward someone, we wanted to boost sales. The facts are it was their job to get the financial referrals any way and we somehow ended up being the bad guys."

"Never again", she said, "never again."

Follow the plot Hazel

My last story on this topic was told to me by Hazel.

Her business was around 9 years old at the time. She had an administration department of 11 people and a great Admin Manager, Cheryl, who had been with her for the past 6 years.

Cheryl had two very young children and she had organised flexible working with Hazel that suited everyone concerned.

One day Cheryl asked Hazel whether they could have a chat.

I'll let Hazel take over.

"It started like any other chat, you know the niceties, and then Cheryl started to tell me about her Mother's cousins' best friends brother Mother, or something like that I'm still not sure. I was trying to follow the path of the events Cheryl was describing, how someone had terminal cancer and how this impacted on this other person and then this impacted on this other person."

"I then started to think, hold on minute, why is she telling me this? She continued and the last few words were, and because of this my Mother will not be able to look after my children anymore and therefore I need to leave."

"You can imagine my surprise. Someone who I don't know has cancer and via some convoluted connection this has an impact on me. I asked Cheryl when she wanted to leave, and she said today. The illness was so aggressive that everyone needed to act quickly."

"My mind was in a blur. If I said no you cannot leave now, how would this look, some poor woman has terminal cancer? If I said yes then who would run the office?"

"Of course I said yes, and then my problems started. For the next 3 months I managed the office whilst I tried to recruit a replacement for Cheryl. I didn't have a business for 3 months, I had a job."

"The recruitment didn't go at all well and I ended up having 3 replacements in the next 12 months until eventually I stumbled upon Gordon, who is still the Office Manager".

If you wanted me to add another thousand similar stories I could, unfortunately they are not isolated, it is just that they are just not generally in the public domain.

You're still not buying it are you? The voice in your head is telling you that for every "bad" story about employees that there are probably a thousand "good" ones that are simply not mentioned. There are not, getting by is not the same as good or even the same league as great.

Maybe out of everyone that I have ever met I have a confirmation bias towards this and seek out these stories? I don't.

Maybe the message is that life is full of surprises and these stories represent a test of your resolve and dedication? You're barking up the wrong tree.

Maybe Liam was wrong about how he thought his staff might behave, maybe Jenny was deluded and she wasn't a great boss, maybe Debbie and Mark were poor at communicating and created their own problem and maybe Hazel should have been better at succession management.

The truth is that when you employ someone you end up employing their entire family and other people you will never get to know. These unseen people will have an impact on your business. The impact will not be as big as the people you employ, but it will be felt and it will hurt.

Some businesses have to have staff and maybe yours is one of these in which case please please please learn from the mistakes of others.

Liam still has a successful business; he has been going well over 20 years now. His employees don't know what he truly thinks about them, he has no particular desire to share this with them.

Liam left school at 16 with virtually no academic qualifications. He had over 30 different jobs until he settled for a small number of years working as a Salesman for manufacturing business. He was good at it; however, he decided that he could make a lot more money by starting his own business and stealing the best customers from his employer.

Liam knew how slaves felt because he was one of them. He knew that slaves didn't care because he didn't.

Liam didn't have the choices that you and I have had; he couldn't have had a career and ended up as a Corporate Executive.

He understood the small business world and he has been successful as a business owner for over 20 years. His staff like him, he is loyal, he is not a caricature of a mean spirited business man he is pragmatist and a realist. He fully understands that it is what he does that makes a difference and not who he is.

I am not suggesting that you never employ anyone but being prepared and having strategies in place will mitigate the consequences when something inevitably goes wrong.

This book is interactive. To access more content for free please visit www.**sufian.me/keepcalm**

Chapter 4.1 – How did you work that out?

You've decided to employ staff, so now we have to take a look at the true cost of employing someone. It is a bit like suggesting that the cost of owning a car is the price of a gallon of petrol and then working out the cost per mile, a foolish thing to do, in your business it could prove to be very dangerous.

People talk in terms of salary £30k per annum or in hourly rates £15 per hour. Invariably we get paid and we pay people every month.

You decide to employ someone for a basic salary of £20,800 per annum. We are going to look at how this relates to a cost to you per hour of work.

I am going to work through an example and here are my assumptions. I apologise for the numbers that are about to appear, these are irrelevant, the real value is in understanding directionally the point I am making.

- There is a 40 hour working week spread over a 5 day week (mon-fri)
- The hourly rate advertised for this job is £10 per hour
- There are 5 weeks annual paid leave
- There are a further 9 paid National Bank Holidays
- The average sickness for your industry is 7 days per year
- Employers cost (tax and National Insurance) are equivalent to 10%. There are some countries in Europe who have rates in multiples of this.

The £20,800 is simply divided by 52 (the number of weeks in the year), divided by 40 (the number of hours to be worked each week), to give £10 per hour.

First of all let us work down the facts, with some minor assumptions.

Out of 52 weeks there are 5 weeks lost to annual holiday. This leaves 47 weeks. A further 9 days are lost to bank Holidays and a further 7 days lost to annual average sickness. This now takes us down to 43 weeks and 4 days or 219 days.

So for 219 days of attending work you will pay £20,800 plus employer's costs of £2,080 (10% of £20,800) = £22,880.

The hourly rate is now £22,880 ÷ (219 x 8) = £13.06

So the hourly rate is now £13.06 or too put it another way over 30% higher than advertised hourly rate, but were not finished yet. This is the small stuff.

If the function that this person carries out is vital to the day to day running of your business, who will do this when they are not there? Will this add real cost to the business or will it be even worse and generate an opportunity cost by taking someone else from their role whilst providing cover?

In any 8 hour day, how many hours is someone productive?

If they work on a manufacturing plant and their workload is decided by the manufacturing process then they are probably productive 70-80% of the time. If however they are knowledge workers this productivity drops enormously.

Imagine that the average effective work they did for you each day was 4 hours, would that be reasonable? In my experience the true answer to this is nearer 2 hours per day. If that person really had to could they get the work done in 2 hrs and to the same if not higher quality?

If they had to get the work done in 2 hrs how well organised would you have to be?

I am going to run with my 2 hours per day and assume that you employ knowledge workers.

This quadruples your cost per hour from £13.06 to a whopping £52.24; we'll round this to £50 per hour for the sake of simplicity.

We advertised a vacancy with an hourly rate of £10 per hour; it has ended up costing us over £50 per hour or 5 times as much!

My point is this, whether my assumptions are valid or not depends on a lot of factors. The real question is am I in the right ball park? The answer is that I am.

You have options when sub-contracting your labour. You can outsource it; this is often off putting because this will normally be quoted at an hourly rate. Without having the benefit of the example we just worked through if you were approached by a sub-contractor to carry out the work for you at £20 per hour you would have probably have said no.

You have a choice, you are creating and you have to decide what activities are critical to your success and those that are not.

We haven't event discussed the time, effort and procedures it takes to employ someone directly and the associated costs of Health & Safety and tools to carry out the job.

You could share a resource with another small company, you could even trade services. There are no fixed rules.

You are the King; make the best decisions for you, and your business.

Chapter 4.2 – Don't talk to the hand

The labour market has changed beyond recognition. Again with my UK hat on I want to paint a picture on how much the labour market has changed.

Before the First World War the labour market in the UK was split roughly like this. I know this is not completely accurate; it is broadly accurate and helps me illustrate a point.

A third of the workforce worked on the land.

A third of the workforce worked in factories.

A third of the workforce was in service (think Downtown Abbey).

A very small percentage was professionals, Doctors and Lawyers etc.

The majority of the work was carried out using muscle power, blue collar workers. A person's major asset was there physicality.

These days the picture has changed dramatically.

Agriculture in the UK accounts for less than 1% of the workforce. Manufacturing is less than 10% and the service sector is now over 80%.

The changes have happened for a variety of reasons, if you want to read about this further there are lots of resources available. I am not an expert on this. My focus is looking at the trend and trying to work out what impact this will potentially have in the future.

One of the biggest impacts is that today someone's knowledge is their biggest asset in the job market. Years ago blue collar workers were suffering from competition in the Global marketplace and now it is the turn of white collar or knowledge workers.

What does this probably mean to you?

Think about it, if you need highly skilled knowledge workers you have a worldwide market place to choose from. The ability to connect and collaborate with these individuals and small companies will only improve and increase year on year.

The Internet is still a baby, growing rapidly but still an infant. An almost endless supply of both knowledge based workers, goods and services as well as potential customers.

You are a King; you are a creator. Do your research into your options and then act.

Chapter 4.3 – Why you suck at interviewing

Before you get all self-righteous on me let me make you feel better by explaining that "you" means everyone.

We all like to think that we are good judges of character.

We all like to think that we are good at listening and objective in our decision making.

There is a fundamental flaw. As human beings are brains developed over 100's of thousands of years, if not millions, until around 100,000 years ago when Homo Sapiens evolved.

Our modern day brain didn't just appear overnight and neither did the ancient brain structure of our ancestors disappear.

The oldest part of our brains control emotions and decision making. Any animal when introduced to a new stimulus needs to decide whether to eat it, fight/flight or mate with it, although we would like to believe otherwise we are still animals and not highly modified machines.

The really interesting part is that the section of our brain that deals with decision making and emotion has no capacity for communication. At this stage of our development we didn't need this capability.

Choose your favourite colour. Have you got one in mind?

Now what quality about this colour appeals to you? How would you describe the colour?

Blue might conjure up conservatism and reliability. Red on the other hand might be dangerous and exciting. Black might be ubiquitous and mysterious. Gold could be warm, rich and luxurious.

I could go on and on. How did you do?

Remember that there is no connection between our emotions and decision making with communication.

You may well have had an emotional response and you may have decided that you have a particular colour, but do you really believe the answer that you gave, do you?

The answer that you gave was logical. The answer that you gave was communicated.

There is no connection what so ever between your favourite colour and your description of it.

You are an intelligent human being living in the 21st century. You are used to voicing your opinions. You are accustomed to answering questions and wanting to continue the charade that you have put thought into your choices and the way to do this is to communicate them eloquently.

You, like everyone else, have a need to preserve your own self-image.

Think about this carefully as this will impact enormously on many areas of your business.

You, and everyone that you have ever met, or will ever meet, make decisions and have emotional responses to these decisions. Everyone then proceeds to communicate their reasons for making decisions in an attempt to give meaning to their actions.

Sometimes the reasons are so articulate and beautifully scripted that we are all taken in.

The last time you were introduced to someone and you only had the briefest of exposure to them you will have formed an opinion. You will have had an emotional reaction and you will have made a decision as to whether this person was "nice" and you felt comfortable with them or the contrary was true and there was "just something about them, but I can't put my finger on it".

Does this sound familiar? I know it does.

You might have articulated it differently. You might have had an experience when someone tells that another person has done something really bad. Your reaction would be "I don't know what it is about them but I just had this "gut" feeling".

When I first came across this idea that there was no connection between my emotions and decisions and how I communicate them I felt great. Without this information I thought I was walking to the beat of a different drum and the entire population had an ability that had just eluded me.

Let me explain.

As a Senior Manager I was often involved in interviewing, sometimes on my own but often as a part of a panel. One memorable day I was part of a panel interviewing for a senior position.

The process went as follows. The candidates had already had a first interview, the usual personality profiling (I will discuss this later) and our job was to listen to a presentation and then ask questions.

We had a scoring card for each candidate that was collected after each presentation.

Over the course of a long day we had seen 6 candidates. When the last candidate had finished and left the room we settled down, after handing in our score cards, and had a chat about how the day had gone.

The discussion then turned to who we thought should get the job; we were in unanimous agreement that it should be Annabel.

The person organising the interviews, from Personal / Human Resources (I'm not sure what you call the department these days) came in and had collated all our scores.

We had decided that Paul should get the job; we all looked at each other, "Paul?", "which one was he?" We were given his picture and his file.

We asked for our original score cards to be given back to us, we altered them and made sure that Annabel came out on top.

The process was transparent, it just didn't work.

Our combined emotional brains had all wanted to give the job to Annabel, but the introduction of this logical scoring system had skewed everything.

I came away happy. It wasn't just me who couldn't interview. I am hopeless at it.

Your "gut" is your way of telling you what decision you should make. It is an emotional response. It is all the years of experience, all the years' preconceptions and biases all rolled into one. Your subconscious trying to help you out, but it cannot speak.

Your "gut" may help you to make a decision, but when recruiting it still has a very low hit rate of success.

You are the King, understanding how people make decisions is really important.

You are the King, understanding how you make decisions is priceless.

Chapter 4.4 – Make me an offer I can't refuse

You are going to recruit, so let's look at some options to improve your chances of success and reduce the amount of time, effort and money you can waste on this area.

There are two ways to lose money very quickly when running your own business (given that your product/service is good and there are people who want to pay for this at a rate that can generate a desired profit) these are **marketing** (specifically advertising) **and employing people**.

So how will you recruit staff?

There are various options out there that you could adopt.

You could rely on word of mouth; someone you know and trust recommends someone to you. This can be very successful however always remember that you are the decision maker, you are the King and this is your business.

Have you ever had a very close friend recommend a film that you "simply must see" and you watch it in disbelief as this juvenile, one dimensional piece of tripe flashes before your eyes?

What went wrong? Your friend, irrespective of how well you know them and how close you are, is not you. They had an emotional response to a film which simply didn't resonate with you.

The down side or risk to you was very inconsequential. Employing someone purely on a recommendation and getting it wrong could have an enormous downside both for your business and even maybe for the relationship between you and your friend. If it doesn't work out they could either feel guilty or angry about the outcome, something you really don't need to be having to concern yourself with.

This is not to say that recommendations do not work out, they can work out fine, just make sure that you carry out the same processes and manage the person in the same way as you would for anyone else, irrespective of how they came to work for you.

You could use the services of a Recruitment Consultant or Agency. This is possibly the most expensive route to recruiting someone. They can charge up to 20% of the first year's salary as a fee and some charge for benefits such as company cars as well.

They will advertise the position, sift through CV's (resumes) and carry out preliminary interviews. Some can also arrange for psychometric tests to be carried out.

This might be the perfect solution for you.

The down side with this approach, and there are many, is that having paid out a substantial fee for the services it will be natural to relate this to the newly recruited member of staff. The tendency might be to be more lenient, to give them more time to settle in.

The cost of keeping anyone in your business that is either not contributing or actually harming your business is almost impossible to put a cost on, so once again treat them the same way as anyone else.

One of the challenges with using outside Consultants is that you have to select ones to work with, another decision that could have a large impact on the people who are made available to you and the end result.

If you don't believe in the ability of people to be able to make effective and rational decisions about how someone will perform in a particular role then why on earth would you employ someone who tells you that they are professionals at this?

You could advertise the position yourself online on any number of portals for a relatively small fee. These days, depending on the type of person you are looking for, you could use social media to help you find someone.

Some organisations don't decide to recruit one person for a particular position they take a different approach. They decide to take on anyone with a pulse and a desire to work for them.

These organisations normally pay commission only for sales people. They don't need to spend hours thinking about decisions on recruitment. They have an evolutionary process in place. They recruit 10 people, there really is only one job, all of the candidates say that they want the job, they all say that they are committed and that they will work hard, they all have a chance to prove it.

The process doesn't take long to sift out the weak from the strong, the ones with the appropriate skills to those who are floundering. It is survival of the fittest or the survival of the best suited.

The organisation is not trying to "develop" people who do not have the potential or capability or aptitude to succeed. They really do believe that talk is cheap and actions are what matter. The rewards are high and visibly, this is why this approach works. The Sales Director drives an expensive and flash car and takes exotic and 5 star holidays, that type of organisation.

These organisations accept that the "interview process" is flawed and ineffective and have decided to deal with it in a pragmatic way.

Even with a highly motivated set of candidates, willing to work for nothing, the success rate is painfully small. This doesn't matter to the organisation or to the next successful person who can be used as a role model for the next intake. If they only hit 1 in 50, that's ok and still worth adopting this method.

A few years ago I worked with a company that carried out psychometric tests for companies when they were recruiting executives. The company employed around a dozen people; as you can imagine they always carried out psychometric tests on anyone that they would consider employing for themselves.

Over a period of around 12 months they recruited 3 new staff. Each one of these recruits caused concerns and each one of them ended up leaving the business after a few painful and in some cases destructive months.

The only topic of conversation with the owners was these new recruits, who did not overlap each other during their employment with the company.

They firmly believed in the value of psychometric testing as part of the selection process. The facts are that their process failed quite spectacularly and had far reaching consequences for the owners, the other employees and ultimately the business for around an 18 month period before they got back on track again.

They continue to use the same process to this very day.

So far we have looked at how you make people aware of the vacancy you have and the different methods of selection that are open to you.

If we turn our attention to actions you can take to maximise the opportunity that you have the best chance of recruiting the best person possible and also mitigating the downside if this turns out to be the wrong decision.

Firstly, if someone is brought to your attention as a possible candidate and you like what you see on paper or what you have heard about them then arrange to have a short telephone conversation with them.

This is relatively easy to do, take up very little time and avoids a sometimes unnecessary first interview.

Be very clear on what your objective is and write down questions that you want to ask. Imagine that the annual salary for this person is sitting in cash on the table in front of you. That is what is at stake; do they deserve to have a shot at getting their hands on this?

If you feel that you would like to take this further, and you must ask them this question as well, and then arrange to meet them.

At this first meeting get them to do something that doesn't relate to their previous role or the role you have in mind. Set them a problem that requires them to use their initiative and to think.

An example of this as follows: There is a local Cinema and for 1 week you are going to be put in charge. The Cinema has 4 screens and each screen has a capacity of 400 people. What do you think the average revenue is for a week?

Give them a set time to carry out the exercise and then question them on how they came up with their answer. This will tell you a lot about them and help your emotions, your gut to lean further one way or another.

The next step will not always be possible, but if it is then ask.

Ask them to make you an offer that you cannot refuse that will help you to say yes to them.

Ask them to come in and work for half a day, a day or a week. As I mentioned sometimes this is just not possible, but if it is that it is invaluable for both of you.

How do they react at the possibility, especially if you cannot see any reason why they would not take up this offer?

Dennis ran a manufacturing business with around 20 people in a very busy office. All the telephone calls coming into the office from customers were enquiries as the company did not carry out any tele sales activity.

Dennis interviewed a young guy called Chris who had just finished University with a First Class Honours Degree in English. During the interview it became apparent that Chris was also very capable and confident with new technology.

Chris explained that he was stuck in a Catch-22 situation. He couldn't get a job because he had no experience and he couldn't get any experience because he didn't have a job.

Dennis asked Chris to make him an offer he couldn't refuse. Come into work the following Monday for the day. If everything worked out fine then there was no reason why Chris wouldn't be offered the position.

Dennis sensed that not all was well when he mentioned this option by Chris' demeanour; however, he pushed the point in an attempt to help Chris. He offered to pay for his expenses.

They agreed and Chris came to work the following Monday. Dennis was out of the office so left his Office Manager, Rachael, to deal with Chris.

Half way thru the morning Dennis received a call from Rachael.

"We have a problem with Chris, he will not pick up the phone" she went on further to explain that whilst Chris was very articulate, intelligent and very personable he was frightened to death of speaking to strangers and therefore would not pick up the phone. He was told repeatedly that he wasn't there to try and sell to them, simply take a message. This didn't help.

Dennis agreed with Rachael to tell Chris to go home, he didn't even make it until lunch time. The job in the office involved answering the phone.

Dennis was very philosophical about this and quite pleased that he had found out this before making a very bad decision to hire Chris and also that Chris realised that he wasn't suited to this type of work.

If a trial is possible, then you are in a much better position to be able to make an informed decision based on observation rather than just trusting what someone is telling you.

However the decision has come about, you have decided to employ someone.

Your offer will probably be subject to suitable references.

You must take up references. If you can speak to the previous employers, the smaller the organisation the better the chance you will have of receiving accurate and valuable human feedback, then arrange for this. Failing the spoken option you should receive written feedback.

If there are any cracks in the references then act.

At all times be aware of what your legal obligations are with regard to employment law, seek advice from qualified professionals and then make your decision.

The references are fine then we move on to the next stage, normally a probationary period of 3 months. Within this period employees will exhibit their true potential and impact, it might just be that you either are not paying attention or you fail to act.

It is critical that you have reviews and feedback in this period. That it is crystal clear what is expected in their role.

Remember when you were at School, how neat the first page in a new exercise book was. The first few days and weeks are that first page. This should be as good as it is going to get as far as attitude is concerned.

If there are any alarm bells in this honeymoon period then act and act quickly, do not store up a problem for later.

Let's take a look at the sporting world, football (soccer) to be more precise and how they recruit footballers.

Professional Football Clubs employ scouts to go and watch players and report back to the Manager. The Manager has the option to go and watch the player in question perform.

Think about this, the ability to see someone do their job, what talent they have, how hard they work, how they relate to the team and the fans.

If the Footballer is a striker then there are statistics that can be scrutinised, the Manager could have more information about the player than the player does.

Virtually all Professional Games are now televised making the observation of an identified existing professional even easier.

Footballers are also quite neatly put together in sub-sets or types. Goalkeepers, full backs, centre backs, holding midfielders, attacking midfielders, strikers etc.

This is in effect the role that they play in the team.

If we imagine a world where Managers do not have the opportunity to ever see a player play, they only have the players' word for how great they are what would happen?

This is possibly the case of someone who hasn't broken into the first team yet and has not played professional football, or is too young at the moment and in which case you are trying to identify what potential this player will have in a number of years' time.

The Manager would sit and listen, ask the player what their best position is and then bring them in for a trial. An opportunity at first hand to see them play and how they perform and also to decide what the Manager thinks their role (best position) could be in their team.

A trial just makes perfect sense doesn't it?

Where there are well known professionals with substantial track records who move from one club to another you would think that this recruitment process is always a success, how could it not be?

Once again the success rate is variable, some of the biggest and best resourced clubs in the world have paid millions and sometimes tens of millions for players that have just not fitted in, not performed and in some cases only played a handful of first team games for their new club.

This is the most transparent recruitment process as one could imagine with clearly defined roles in an environment with identical rules and yet there is still a great opportunity for failure.

Your process will probably not be as transparent, the role will most probably be slightly different and the organisation and culture will definitely be different. These extra variables again increase the possibility of failure.

You need the staff; you made this decision when you made the choice of the business you wanted.

Make sure that your business is excellent at managing human resources at all times. If you are to have a number of staff and you do not possess the necessary inter-personal skills to manage people effectively then you will need someone who has these skills.

Staff issues never go away in a small business, they never fix themselves. Intervention and management is required and ultimately as the King this is your responsibility.

You are the King; be firm, be clear and understand that people want to be slaves in your Kingdom.

Chapter 4.5 – Please get off the bus

Imagine that you have a work force of 10 people and that just one of these people is giving you cause for concern, for whatever reason. It is almost impossible to begin to imagine what impact this could have on your business.

Firstly this is 10% of your entire workforce, not just one person.

Secondly, because you are small there should have been a very good reason why this person was employed doing the role that they are carrying out.

Thirdly, managing people takes time, recruiting, training, holidays, performance managing and dealing with any personal issues.

Lastly, the emotional stress of dealing with people when things are not going well cannot be emphasised enough. You have someone who is potentially destroying your dream, deflecting your precious time away from working on your business rather than working in your business. You can feel the impact that they are having on other employees and they are the subject of virtually every conversation you have with friends and advisors about your business.

You want to be the best boss possible, so you try everything you can. You assume the position of responsibility; after all you decided to employ them. You do not hold them to the same standard that you would expect from yourself if you were an employee, and above all you excuse their behaviour and performance.

You see this as a learning curve and think that perhaps you are doing something wrong and if you work at it hard enough you will develop the skills that will help this person to contribute effectively to your business.

You are wrong and wasting valuable energy.

You need to make a simple decision that people who work for you are either on the bus or off the bus. They are either with you or they are not. They are either assets of the business or assassins of the business. There is no half way house. There is no "just getting by", you deserve better and you should demand better for yourself.

We are human beings and if we are caring human beings we will struggle with decisions to let people go, to sack them, to make them redundant.

You may have seen this happen in large corporations many times, either personally been involved or affected or just been a distant spectator on the news. It seems very impersonal, almost like a machine or the machinery of the business is taking the decision.

With your business the decision is personal, it is your decision and that is partially why people find this so hard to do. They will suffer and excuse year after year an underperforming employee. They know what they really should do, but they never get around to it.

These "bad apples" can be like a cancer in your business. If you were constantly letting down a customer what would happen? They would find a new supplier.

Get advice and make that difficult decision.

Go to bed and imagine that you are making that difficult decision the next day. When you wake up look at yourself in the mirror, do you feel "lighter" or "heavier"?

If you feel "lighter" then deep down you know that this is the correct thing to do, if you feel "heavier" there are still some unresolved issues and maybe you are not striking at the root cause of these.

A few years ago I was involved with a group of business owners who all employed staff, mainly in manufacturing. It was a safe place where we could all share what was on our minds and get feedback and support from each other, a sort of mastermind group.

Every single person had people issues, some of whom were other Directors of the businesses. As each person relayed their own story it became evident that each us were struggling to make a decision, to try to performance manage, to provide excuses and yet a roomful of experienced like-minded people immediately offered the advice "get rid".

We understood each other's pain and turmoil and the impact this was having.

The question was asked "Has anybody ever been in this situation and made the decision to part with someone and then regretted that they hadn't made this decision earlier"?

Everyone agreed that this was always the case.

Make your decision and make it as quickly as is possible given your particular set of circumstances at the time.

Having employees and making difficult decisions just go hand in hand. This needn't ever make you callous or jaded about people it is just that you are focused on what is best for your customers and your business.

You are the King, your decision is final.

This book is interactive. To access more content for free please visit www.sufian.me/keepcalm

Chapter 5
Step 5: Get great at Marketing or die. This is the reality of modern day business

Chapter 5.0 – Life's not fair

You understand that life is not fair, who said it would be?

Some people are more intelligent than you, some are better looking than you and others are richer than you, ok you get my point I'll stop.

In the small business world the single and most meaningful area where you simply must understand fairness is in Marketing.

This is an area where you cannot even try to bend the will of the world in your direction simply because you feel that you deserve the attention. You will die trying.

The products that we end up buying are the ones that we are aware of. They are not necessarily the best available products or services. Over a period of time we can be convinced that they are the best as maybe some of the other better products failed to survive or we are still not aware that they exist. We are now attached to our choices and the risk of changing is too great.

Your job is simple. **Firstly you accept that businesses that are great at Marketing succeed. Secondly, your business becomes great at Marketing.**

If you are a highly technical person you will be able to point out all the flaws in a competitor's product and all the reasons why your product is better. You might have inside knowledge about these competitor products and feel aggrieved at how poor their quality is, right from design, manufacture and customer service.

What you think, know and feel at this stage has no impact on customers. They only know what they are aware of and they need to be aware of you if you are going to make your business a success.

I will use a story from one of the big boys to illustrate a point. Apple is one of the world's biggest companies, most people would credit Apple with inventing the tablet (IPad), and the truth is they didn't. Most believe that Apple is great at innovating new technology. It is not its biggest strength and virtually all of Apple's flagship products are based upon technology developed by someone else.

Apple is great at understanding consumers and how they interact with technology and Apple is great at Marketing.

It is easy for us to believe and create our own myth around Apple. This matters not one jot to Apple's loyal customers or to me. I use this to illustrate a point; it pays to get great at Marketing.

As the King you will be head of Marketing or make it your mission to find a champion to take on this critical role.

Chapter 5.1 – Close enough to kiss

Most people think of Marketing in terms of advertising; the visible side of marketing that they are used to seeing and consuming.

The advertising could be TV, Radio, Newspaper, Magazines, Direct Mail, Trade Shows, Flyers, Internet, PR and Sponsorship etc.

Marketing includes advertising, however it is much more than this.

The best definition to Marketing I have ever heard is this. "Marketing is getting someone close enough to kiss".

The actual kiss is the sale.

In this definition of marketing any part of your business that may come into contact with a potential customer is part of your Marketing.

This means that the way you or your staff answer the telephone, the look of your website, the clothes staff wear, the appearance of any vehicles that you have, the pricing of products, the tone of emails, your letterheads, your social media presence as well as advertising is part of your Marketing.

The vast majority of people do not start a business wanting to market products or services. It is not a skill that they have or that they understand or are comfortable with. The truth is that without this in your business you will always be getting less than you really deserve and in yours eyes some people will be get much more than they deserve.

Most business owners I have ever met treat Marketing as a bit of a side issue, something they will get around to. Often they cannot see the value in it because they do not understand it.

The customer is now King; they have more choice than ever before.

As a King yourself you have to accept certain realities exist and deal with them accordingly.

Chapter 5.2 – How did customers become Kings?

This is an interesting and very recent journey that you must understand in order to plan how you will Market your products and services.

There are millions of businesses out there who have not woken up to the new reality and are still banging away following old strategies and tactics to get customers. Some of them are questioning why this is not working anymore; some are just throwing more resources at this and working harder for the same or smaller returns.

I attended a seminar recently when a member of the audience, who were are all small business owners, stood up and recounted how she had rang a customer 27 times before he eventually agreed to a meeting and this had led to a large order.

She almost got a standing ovation, there were cheers and the organiser at the front gave her a wonderful endorsement and held her up as a role model of what can be achieved.

I sat watching all this unfold and wanted to vomit.

People would be leaving and going back to their businesses the next day with the "try harder" maxim and eventually we will succeed. They were totally missing the reality of the situation and taking the information at face value without engaging brain or considering alternative options.

The woman who got up and spoke had a victory, she won the lottery. I am pleased for her. How did she do this? Perseverance was the key, never giving up.

You will see this message of perseverance often cited when you research the world of Entrepreneurs and business start-ups. What it doesn't take into account are firstly all the people who did just that, persevered, and still failed. It also doesn't tell you what the cost of that perseverance were to the success.

In the case of the woman who after 27 calls got her meeting how many other calls were made to other people that did not result in a happy ending? Could this be a hundred calls, a thousand, maybe 10,000 or maybe even

100,000?
I don't have the answer to this and it is academic.
Customers do not want to be hunted and we do not want to be hunters.

Years ago there was very little choice for a consumer compared to today.

We will follow the story of Alice, the year is 1987. Alice lives in a town in the middle of the country. The town has a high street with a number of shops, there are two shoe shops.

Alice has dreamt of getting a pair of Ruby Slippers, she likes dancing and has been chosen for the part of Dorothy in a local amateur production of The Wizard of Oz.

She excitedly visits the high street only to find that neither of the two shoe shops have any Ruby Slippers.

Her next attempt is to visit the local City; this is 45 minutes away by car. The high street there has half a dozen shoe shops. Once again Alice is in for disappointment as none of the shops stock anything remotely like the slippers that Alice is searching for.

Eventually her dance teacher has an idea and shows Alice a catalogue, specifically for the theatre productions, and Alice finds her Ruby Slippers. They are very expensive; almost three times the price of similar slippers in other colours that she could buy in the shops. She decides to purchase them and 3 weeks later the Ruby Slippers arrive.

Unfortunately the Ruby Slippers are too small and Alice has to send them back, but eventually after another 4 weeks she receives her Ruby Slippers and they fit perfectly. Alice is overjoyed and can't wait for opening night.

We now move forward to the present day. Alice wants some Ruby Slippers. She enters what she wants onto a search engine (Google, Bing, Yahoo etc.) and selects local stockists. Within seconds she can see which stores have them in stock, what the prices are, what the sizes are and what other customers are saying about them.

Alice also has the option to order the Ruby Slippers online and they will be delivered the next day.

As there is not a big market for Ruby Slippers Alice never had the opportunity to come into contact with any information or adverts about Ruby Slippers in 1987. If she had come into contact it would have been for probably the largest National supplier and not a local one and would have not been a convenient purchase filled with choice.

Today Alice is the King. She lets the market know what she wants and invites them to show her what they have. Alice is giving her permission for businesses to market to her and then she will make a decision.

This kind of permission marketing has been a revolution, it might have been a silent revolution but make no mistakes it has been a revolution. It is just that most of us; most of the time takes it for granted.

In the past businesses would "interrupt" you with their advertising (I am using this as opposed to the full definition of Marketing). They would attempt to send out a broadcast message and hope that some of the people that received the message would be their target market.

During a football (soccer) match on TV at half-time there would be advertisements for Lager, there still are. The adverts would be aimed at men, so the women and children watching are being part of the audience viewing figures that determine the cost of advertising but are not the target market.

Any men that don't drink lager and would never do so are also seeing the adverts.

This is a broadcast, this is an interruption. You sat down to watch a football (soccer) game and now someone is trying to sell you lager or entertain you with an advert to strengthen their brand.

Imagine that you sell Sushi and you have paid to have access to 60,000 supporters who will attend an event an arena. You stand outside the arena, along with various competitors selling hot-dog, burgers, pies etc. who have also paid to access these people. You shout at people walking past letting them know that you have Sushi.

How many people out of the 60,000 are hungry? How many of the 60,000 know what Sushi is? How many of the 60,000 know that you are there?

The chances are that you will not have many customers, but you have had potential access to 60,000 people.

This would be the same if you were advertising in a magazine or paper.

Now let's imagine that everyone at the event has been told that Sushi is available and if they want to know more they can take a leaflet with your details on and where to find you at half-time. This time you will only pay for the people who said they wanted more information.

Out of 60,000 there 500 people who were interested, and out of these 300 bought from you.

Now as far as I am aware this is not how it works at sporting or music events yet, it does however work this way on the Internet.

The customer is the King, the customer does not want to be hunted, they do not want broadcast messages that try and interrupt them.

People can sometimes call this "demand generation" in an attempt to re-brand and to confuse you, it is not demand generation it is broadcast interruption advertising.

You might be thinking that your products and services are not sold via the Internet and you cannot see what relevance this has to you.

The fact that you do not trade via the Internet is irrelevant, people will still research and talk about you or the products and services you provide.

The biggest mistake would be to ignore the great opportunity that is waiting for you. **People out there want your product and they are searching, they want to give you permission to help, support, educate, inform and engage with them.**

You are the King; engage with your people and let them know that you care.

Chapter 5.2 – What does qualified mean?

You have decided that you are going to take marketing seriously and develop a Marketing Plan.

You do not feel that you have the necessary skills to do this yourself so enlist an Agency or you recruit someone.

You decide to take on a Marketing Graduate, you get on very well and they are very bright and full of enthusiasm.

You expected that as part of their degree they would be covering Marketing Plans and The Marketing Mix (Known as either the four P's or 5P's).

As they are young you would expect that they have a good understanding of social media and the latest trends, once again big tick in the box.

The problem is this; they have been studying in readiness to join the Marketing Department of a large company or a Marketing Agency. The world of small business is new to them. The challenges that you face are new to them.

They are not Marketing Plumbers; they are Marketing Engineers with no experience.

An Agency might be a better option, a good one will not be cheap, once again finding a good one who can help you to increase Sales will be hard to find.

I would separate the day to day technical activities of Marketing that might be frightening to you, away from the content you want to create and the audience that you want to reach.

You need to think hard about where you target audience comes together, what else do they buy and where from. What do they buy before your product and after your product?

You are the King; you are qualified to identify and understand your people. Instruct others on how to help you reach your people.

123

Chapter 5.3– All things to all people

Before you take any action on Marketing your products and services you have to be able to articulate quite clearly a number of things.

Firstly, what are the benefits of using this product/service? This is the "why".

Secondly, identify your potential customer? This is the "who".

It is tempting when asked "who this product/service will benefit", to respond with "anyone and everyone". This is normally a recipe for disaster.

The next few sections will help you clarify your thoughts so that you are clear on these critical matters.

You are the King; don't try and please all of the people all of the time.

This book is interactive. To access more content for free please visit www.**sufian.me/keepcalm**

Chapter 5.4– Look again and now tell me what you see

The last thing that you would wish for your business is to fall into the "so what" category. You see this so often, even after people have put a great deal of time, effort and money into trying to communicate effectively.

Often they are just focused on the wrong things.

Take a few moments and surf the web. Search for products or services that you may not have used before.

I want you to look at business websites with a fresh and intelligent pair of eyes.

Get past the colour schemes and exotic designs, it is not important whether you like this or not. What do you see? What are they telling you? What do they want you to do?

Try looking up local businesses that you know, if they have one, does the website represent what you feel about them?

How are we doing? Let me help you.

Try searching for local Accountants, they will tend to have a website, are professionals run by qualified educated people and they will probably not have anything for you to buy.

The vast majority will tell you "what" they do. They will definitely tell you about themselves and that they were established in 1650 etc.

So the first thing to notice is that much of the focus and language will be inward looking, about them and not about you.

Some of them will tell you "how" they do what they do. They might want to tell you how they operate a personal service and get to understand each and every client as a person etc.

Now so far if you had to select an Accountant from what you've seen how would you decide?

We are so sophisticated these days that our response most of the time is "so what". We do it faster, cheaper, better quality, and still want to say so "so what".

Do any of the Accountants' websites describe "why" they are in business? My guess is that they don't.

Remember that we make emotional decisions, not logical ones. The "what" we do and "how" we do it are all logical; never striking at our emotions and never making a connection. Do you get the impression that these companies really understand what is like to run your own business and have communicated their "why"?

I haven't come across one that does, if you have well done.

You were close enough to kiss, you were on their website and they wasted all that hard work.

In the future look at other business websites differently, they are a great source of both what not to do and also how to get it right. The majority get it wrong; you cannot afford to be one of these.

You are the King; you must communicate simply, effectively and without ego. People want to hear from you, they want to know the "why" and not just the "what" and the "how".

Chapter 5.5 – The $64,000 question

This is not my question; I wish it was because it is pure genius.

Anyone who has ever undergone any basic sales training will tell you about features and associated benefits. They will tell you that benefits have to be relevant and they will tell you how in large organisations the Marketing Department often provides marketing Material full of features.

I have a pen in front of me; it has fluting down the sides. This is a feature. The benefit is that the pen is easy to hold and will not slip.

I could have said that the pen is ergonomically designed to give you the most comfortable writing experience ever.

If you have never come across this concept before then have some fun and try it out, remember that the benefits have to be relevant to your target audience.
Pick any object and start with a feature and then provide a relevant benefit.

Another way of describing this is sell the "sizzle" and not the "steak".

If you were selling drill bits the "sizzle" would be the hole that is achieved by using your drill bits. You could take this further and say that the hole will have a bracket that allows for a sentimental picture to be mounted on it.

So we start with drill bit and end up with a proud and happy couple staring at a beautiful picture of their wedding day, you get the idea.

You will notice this kind of thing everywhere now.

The alternative would be to describe how durable the drill bit is because it has a tungsten tip and how it will not let you down when you need it.

The $64,000 question revolves around this. You need to understand what the true benefit of your product or service is, from this you can decide how and what to communicate.

The question follows shortly. You must understand that being able to think about this and come up with an answer that you believe in will have a profound effect on you and your business.

If this takes you minutes to answer you are almost without doubt barking up the wrong tree. The first time I tried this it took almost 3 days to come up with my answer.

The question is this: **"If you had God like powers and could guarantee that any users of your product or service derived one benefit from using this, what would it be?"**

This is a great question and should make you think, and think deeply.

Once you have your answer then work backwards from this to create a narrative for your business. The majority of your communication should have this in mind. The benefit might end up being the stock answer to "what does your business do?"

As the King you must contemplate many things and prioritise what aspects of your business take centre stage. This subject should be right out in front centre stage at all times.

Chapter 5.6 – The winner is...

Now you know what the benefit of your product or service is you need to figure out who your ideal customers are.

It might be that you have been researching a particular market sector and trying to develop a solution to a problem that they have and don't want or develop a solution that they need and don't have yet.

If this is the case you would do the $64,000 question after you have selected your target market and started at least to develop your product.

You cannot be all things to all people, this way lays disaster. You have to identify a market niche. You have to go deep and not wide.

The fear is that a niche is just that and might be quite small. The major benefit is that this niche wants to be specifically serviced. This niche has particular needs, frustrations and desires. This niche is identifiable; this niche is full of individuals wanting to be treated as an individual and not like the masses.

Make a list of 5 types of businesses or people who you believe would derive most benefit from your product or service.

What do you know about them?

Try and put yourself in their shoes, even better if you can reach some of these with a questionnaire to test out your ideas and ask them what they want.

It is difficult for people to explain what they want. They will use phrases such as "this should be easier", "this shouldn't take as long" "I don't understand why I have to do this" and "this just makes no sense".

You must develop a mind-set where you are constantly thinking about what is in this for the customer. This is easier than it sounds. We tend to look at things through our own minds eye and how things will affect us.

Your business is there to serve others and by doing so you will be rewarded.

Work your way down the list of 5 and narrow this down to just 3.

This is enough to get you started. It can make it easier to think of each one the sectors as a person. This is Jane; she is a 35 year old Teacher. She is single, well-educated and loves foreign holidays. In her spare time she reads and enjoys cycling.

How will Jane react when you try to communicate with her? How should you communicate, what style of language should you use. Where do people like Jane congregate?

Keep investigating and asking questions until you have a clear picture of who your niche market is.

You are the King; you must understand the people so that you can serve them.

Chapter 5.7 – Think before you invest

Large organisations "spend money" in Marketing and Advertising. Their goals are different. They want to achieve brand recognition, brand loyalty and product awareness. The "spending" of money means that they are not expecting, neither will they be able to, to calculate a return on investment (ROI).

You are "investing money & resources" into your Marketing and Advertising. You are not looking to make people aware of you. You want people to buy from you. This investment is like any investment that you make and you must demand a return on investment (ROI). You should be able to track the investment and the returns that it delivers, this means tracking where your customers are coming from, how else will you know whether you are investing in the correct areas?

If you have a website the purpose of the website is to "start a relationship" with a potential customer. If you start believing that you will be able to sell to someone who is surfing on the Internet and finds you, then you are in for a big disappointment. This is just not how people behave.

If a Marketing Plumber tells you that they can get you on page 1 of Google and this will obviously mean that you will generate lots of sales, they are misleading you.

Think of this way, even if they could get you on page 1, without using pay per click (the sponsored ads that appear on Google) then this is only part of the story. Imagine that I have found the perfect spot for your new retail business, it is on the busiest High Street in country, and the footfall is tremendous. This in itself will not generate any sales.

People come into the shop for a look, they were passing by the door anyway, and still no one buys. They do not buy because you do not have what they want, the displays are not attractive enough, your pricing is too high or too low etc.

The Marketing has worked, they are close enough to kiss, but you didn't get the sale. The way you decided to organise yourself only gave you a single chance to convert the visitor into a customer. You only focused on part of the job; the Marketing Plumber will want paying, as you are on page 1 on

Google (for a period of time). You will run out of money, at some point, and realise that you cannot afford the rent.

There are two easy ways to waste money in a small business, one is employing people that you either don't need or do not contribute and the other is paid for advertising.

You are the King; make sure you are investing and not just spending.

Chapter 5.8 – This is what the Big Boys do

When people are trying to get you to spend money they will try to convince you with stories of success from World Class organisations. They will mention Apple, Google, Microsoft, McDonalds, Coca Cola, Facebook, Twitter etc.

The reasons these World Wide Brands are mentioned are numerous, here are a few:

Firstly, the person mentioning these examples wants you to associate him with these blue chip entities.

Secondly, by mentioning the brand it will get awareness and he will not have to explain what the company does or who they are.

Thirdly, as a business owner you are in the same game as these people, you just happen to be a little smaller, for the moment. They can inspire you.

Fourthly, finding these stories is very easy, often it takes seconds.

Lastly, you will think, just like the Marketing Plumber showing you these examples that the same rules apply to you and these brands.

At some stage each of the businesses mentioned was like yours, they were small and no one knew or cared about what they did.

They are World Wide Brands now and they inhabit a different space to you, let me explain.

The first difference is obvious, they have vast assets at their disposal and they can attract the World's Best resources. Compared to you their resources are virtually unlimited, but this is not the biggest difference.

The biggest difference is that they are World Wide Brands and this directly affects how they communicate and Market themselves. The Marketing side is what we should be particularly interested in, understand it and then act accordingly.

Walk down any high street you can think of and with a picture of a coke bottle, without the words on, and ask 100 passer byes to tell you if they recognise the product or company. The hit rate will be high, over 90%.

If you then asked the same people what words or values they associated with this brand, once again the overwhelming majority, would tell you and there would be some common ground within the feedback. Ask the same people to describe a hotel that was built by say Apple and what it would like, even though Apple don't currently build hotels, and once again people would have a clear idea of what It might look like.

The point is that these World Wide Brands do NOT tell consumers what their brand qualities are. Consumers decide what is a brand and what qualities are associated with it.

World Wide Brands do not need to continuously tell people what they do, we already get it, they do however continuously try to support their "brand values" that we gave them and trust them for. If they try and deviate too much it confuses us and we cease to trust them.

Imagine having a good friend, who is quite shy, they never use bad language and never tell jokes. One day you meet for coffee and he is using foul language and telling rude jokes all the time. You would think there was something wrong. This is the same with brands, they need to be congruent.

So the next time when someone relates a story about one of these Brands and what they did in a recent campaign, ask yourself what relevance is this to you?

You are not a brand; the chances are you will never be a brand. You have values, personal and business values. Things that you will and will not do things that you aspire to, you have chosen these; your customers have not given them to you.

Brands can cost £100's of millions per year to support.

You are trying to cut thru the haze and sell products and services to potential clients who do not yet know that you exist.

If you believe you have a brand then you will try to act like a brand, you will lead with your ego and you will lose money. You will want to hear your radio adverts on the local radio and see your face in paid for magazine articles. Your ego will be boosted and your bank balance destroyed.

If you think you are a brand try the high street test, go to Oxford Street in London and ask a 100 people to look at the name of your business and see what response you get and how aware were they. Enough said.

You are the King; you reside over a world of your making.

This book is interactive. To access more content for free please visit www.**sufian.me/keepcalm**

Chapter 5.9 – The future online

I do not have a crystal ball; however, I have developed a strong view on where I believe the future of online will be with regard to small businesses. This view is supported many players who already are advocating this right now.

Before we look forward we should take a look at how we arrived where we are now. In particular I am going to look at Google, simply because they dominate the Internet as far as search is concerned. "Googled" has become a verb and part of our everyday lives.

A few years ago, not that long ago, I was attending an event and there were about 15 business owners all sat around a board table. Someone mentioned something of interest and I said "I will look that up on Yahoo" later. The guy next to me said "Try Google, It's much better", I'd not heard of Google so he, along with just about everybody in the room proceeded to firstly tell me how to spell "Google" and secondly how great it was.

Over the coming months and years, like the vast majority of us, Google became part of my everyday life; at work I was using it every day.

One day I asked this question to myself "how do Google make money?"

I didn't think that I was paying any money to them; they had no visibility on the high street. They were everywhere and yet they didn't exist.

They provided a great service, searching for anything on the Internet became so much quicker and more relevant. I decided to research them.

What I found is that Google made money from advertising. The sponsored links on page one of search results, the design and format has altered slightly, generated revenue for Google.

Every time someone clicked on the sponsored link Google earned money. The business that paid for the sponsored link could set daily limits on spends and place bids to get to the top of the sponsored links in a kind of auction.

Google had revolutionised the industry by delivering results that were highly "relevant". Their entire business model is based upon this. If you searched for something and the results that appear are not relevant you will soon be voting with your feet (or fingertips) and try another search engine.

The other major thing that Google did was attempt to bring some order to the millions of listings on the Internet that would be "relevant" to the search terms you had entered and add a concept of "authority" to these. The more "authority" that your website had the higher Google was going to rank you and the more relevant your content was the higher the possibility that you would appear on page 1.

The easiest way I can describe "authority" is this. You are standing alongside another 99 people. Some of the people there know each other, some don't. You are all experienced Carpenters. One by one you are asked to raise your hand and state your name, when you do this the rest of the people are asked whether they know you or not. The person who has the most people raise their hand to say that they knew them has the most "authority".

Google worked out "authority" on the Internet by studying how many "backlinks" a website had. If other websites had links back to your website, this was classed as other people on the web giving you "authority", a sort of self-generating popularity measure.

So far we have relevancy and authority. The relevancy was a combination of what was visible on your website (on page), and what was not visible (off page). The off page content could be telling Google what your site was about, key words etc.

When people spoke about SEO (Search Engine Optimisation) it was a combination of on page, off page and back links.

Google's "relevancy" has two distinct customer groups that it needs to satisfy. The users, the people who browse allow Google to earn money by providing targeted advertising when these browsers enter search terms.

The businesses bidding for Pay per Click could easily find themselves as the highest bidder but not top of the sponsored links; this is because Google also took relevancy strongly into the equation.

If your website was about Car Insurance and you bid the term "House Insurance" then it was highly unlikely that Google would have your sponsored links shown anywhere. Google was on one hand appearing to turn down the offer to make money from businesses that wanted to advertise with them because the risk was too great to their business model. They have to be relevant or die.

If you didn't pay for sponsored links with Google you would form part of what is called "Organic" listings. This is because your site was relevant, you maybe had back links, good on page and good off page content.

In the early days Google's business model was being attacked and abused, it still is today. People who understood the rules that Google applied to ranking, Google's algorithms, tried to persuade businesses that they could get them to the top of Google's search results.

When this achieved via malicious and underhand means it is referred to as "Black Hat". An example of this could be a facility called "link farms" where companies would create thousands of artificial links back to your site so that Google would give it "authority".

Over the years Google has constantly become more sophisticated and altered how it ranks websites and other content (growth of social media). Google cannot afford to lose this battle, in my opinion it will not lose this battle.

The businesses selling services such as "link farms" were taking revenue away from Google and also potentially impacting the core foundation of "relevancy".

The very early days have passed now; they were a bit like the Wild West.

Imagine the year is 2064 and we are looking back at the turn of the century, what would we think? We would view the Internet at being in its infancy, to compare it with film making we would look it as perhaps the "silent movie era". Some of the foundations were laid down but there were still great innovations to come.

My money is on Google surviving and thriving. The games of SEO manipulation and cheating will have to die and become a thing of the past; this is not the case just yet, but I believe that it is coming.

The current landscape rewards businesses for being relevant, creating

content on various platforms and in widening formats.

Platforms used to be just website and directories. Today there are numerous social media platforms; some companies don't have traditional websites anymore.

Content used to be just text and images, we are about to be flooded with video.

As downloads speeds continue to increase and more and more mobile devices have access to the Internet we will, in some countries we already have, have access to potential customers wherever they are and at any time of day or night.

Once the genie is out of the box it will not be put back.

The way that people market their businesses on the Internet now is sometimes referred to as "Inbound" Marketing.

Inbound Marketing refers to the flow of customers towards a product or service that is driven by content, comments from any source (ex-customers on social media) and is seen to be meeting the wants and needs of customers who are discovering for themselves what they want rather than advertisers telling them what they think they should have.

For a small reputable business this is great news. There are people out there looking for your type of product and service and they do not trust traditional advertising as a way to find what they want.

You have the same barrier to entry as everyone else, irrespective of size.

Often people will tell you that this form of marketing is free, it isn't. It is time consuming to do it correctly and to do enough of it. Another consideration is that if you take to a social media platform and engage directly with your customers then you are creating an expectation that this level of interaction will be consistent and continue.

The danger is that you start down this route, full of enthusiasm, and then decide that you do not have time for it anymore. You will then face a backlash as the people you have let down will voice their opinions.

A reputation takes a long time to develop and can be damaged with a few strokes of a keyboard and a couple of clicks of a mouse.

Social Media – when this phenomenon first emerged I attended various lectures with prominent speakers from the industry to try and get a handle on what was involved and what it would mean for me as a small business owner.

There was lots of excitement around and things were evolving very rapidly.

It boils down to this if you are looking at it from a business perspective.

Social media is another form of communication, an opportunity for you to connect with existing and potential customers. Unlike previous forms of communication this takes place, for most part, publicly.

The tone of the communication is more conversational than formal, more personal than corporate.

The best advice I have ever received about Social media is to be inconsistently consistent, let me explain.

Most people that you know, whilst I am sure they are very engaging and witty, will tell you things that are interesting whilst you are having a coffee together. It will not be a constant stream for every hour of every day that will keep you on the edge of your seat. When they have something to say they think is of interest they will share. They are being consistently inconsistent; this is how you should approach Social media, if you decide to engage with it at all.

When you have something of interest that you want to share then share it, otherwise keep quiet.

I meet many people that are fixated and worried about social media, what to say, where to say it, are they aware of the latest trends, what are the new platforms that are breaking through.

You simply have to ask yourself whether there is a place for Social Media within your Marketing activities that you have identified; can you reach your target market here? If the answer is yes, then decide upon a strategy, you can outsource social media to any number of small organisations. If you do outsource be sure to measure your return on investment.

You are the King; you have a vision for the future, keep it fresh and re-visit your vision regularly. Shiny objects shouldn't concern you.

5.10 – Choose wide and go deep

Now you know who your target market is and what you want to communicate you know have to decide on how you are going to engage with them.

What is appropriate and cost effective for you?

Remember, we do not want to take part in any interruption broadcast marketing activity. You have identified your target and now you need direct response from them.

Wherever you can you should automate the sales process that takes a potential customer on a journey from being interested to buying.

If you want to test an idea and concept quickly you can do this using Google's Pay per Click advertising. Within a day you could have feedback on your products and from real people.

Initially decide upon one single channel and master this rather than trying a broad bush approach and hoping that something will stick.

Eventually you will probably have a number of marketing channel pillars that support your business and help it move forwards. This is not only prudent, avoiding all your eggs all your eggs in one basket, but is also creates the opportunity for transfer of skills from one area to another.

A channel might be, Pay per Click, SEO (Search Engine Optimisation), Direct Mail, Tele-Sales, Trade Shows, Email Campaigns, Networking Events or Social Media Campaigns.

There is no real short cut to success, you have to act and then you have to continually refine your approach to find out what works. Don't fall into the trap of continuing with the exact same approach and expecting a different result.

It is very easy, for example, on the Internet to carry out split testing. An example would be creating a headline and altering one single word. Which headline creates the highest response?

You carry this process out again and again. Anyone who tells you that they have found a way, that you can afford, to create guaranteed marketing messages that will deliver thousands of pre-qualified leads to your door is lying.

Anyone who tells you that they can create a "viral" video that guarantees success is lying.

Do yourself a favour and do the hard work, earn your success. Be in a situation where you can repeat it and model it, don't leave it down to pure chance, don't be in a situation where you have no idea where and why your customers are currently knocking on your door.

You are the King; with such power comes responsibility. Be dedicated and be the best King you could possibly be.

5.11 - Why did you buy this?

I was at an event where the speaker, a great speaker, posted a picture of a black BMW on the screen. There were about 500 people in the audience, mainly professionals.

She asked a question. "Raise your hand if you have a positive association and feelings about this?"

I was sat in the front row; I raised my hand and turned around to see about half of the room do the same.

Once we had put our arms down and there had been a bit of nervous giggling she asked another question.

"Now please raise your hand if you have negative feelings about this, not ambivalent, but negative feelings towards this".

I looked around the room, there was more nervous giggling and gasps as around half of the hands in the room were up again.

When we had settled down, which took quite a bit of time, she continued.

She looked up at the picture of this shining example of German engineering and asked, rhetorically, "What does this mean?"

She continued, "This is an image and yet it created these powerful responses. This image is something that we can all recognise and we know that it is a machine, it doesn't think, it doesn't feel, it has no personality and yet we are projecting, it would appear, these emotions and qualities onto this image."

I have been to thousands of meetings and presentations and out of all of the ones I ever attended this one stood out, and still do, as being very special.

One of things I had been interested in and struggling with is why people buy what they buy. How do they make the choices that they make? If I could figure this out I would find it much easier to run any business.

A few months earlier I had stopped at a fast food outlet whilst travelling on the motorway. I ordered my food and when the young guy behind the counter asked me what drink I would like, I replied that I would like a diet coke. He responded, "We only have Pepsi, is that alright?"

The truth is, as sad as it may sound, it wasn't alright. My heart sank just a little bit. Here was I a mature man, who had worked for years in the food manufacturing industry **getting upset about fizzy water**.

I was a sophisticated buyer, I understood marketing and here I was, without realising it tied to Coca-Cola. How did this happen? Why did this happen? Could I change this? Could I replicate this for myself?

So as I sat in this hall listening to this remarkable presentation I was excited and couldn't wait to see where this was going.

"Could someone who thought that this is a positive image please stand up and explain why", I turned around again and a young guy in his mid-twenties stood up. It turned out he was a Solicitor, he said that the BMW was "Sexy, fast, well-engineered, aspirational and I want one".

"Could someone now stand up who thought that this represented something negative and explain why".

Towards the middle of the room a young woman stood up, once again she was in her mid-twenties, she worked in medical sales. "**I think that anyone who drives one of these devil creations is an arrogant, road hogging, fuel guzzling inconsiderate b*********".

Everyone started laughing.

"How can this be?" asked the presenter. "That this image, this brand, generates such forceful and divergent responses?"

"It cannot be the car itself, it cannot be the message that BMW is trying to convey, and therefore it has to be in the minds of you the audience".

She went on to ask another rhetorical question. "Do you think that BMW should concentrate on continuing to get their messages across to this

145

young guy here or try to convince the young woman to change her opinion?"

"BMW are not interested in this young woman, they are not even going to attempt to try and convert her. The young man on the other hand is a different proposition, he wants a BMW, he aspires to own one and when the day comes when he has a choice between a BMW, a Mercedes or an Audi they want him to choose BMW."

She continued to explore why we interpreted this brand the way that we did and introduced the concept of archetypes.

The very basic theory behind this, first developed by Swiss psychologist Carl S. Jung used the word "archetype" to refer to the recurring patterns found in universal stories, identifying the themes, symbols and imagery as part of the human psyche.

From a Marketing perspective this has been developed into understanding brands as representing a particular common character (archetype) that is identifiable in any culture, such as the warrior or the explorer.

When we encounter these archetypes and they resonate with us they can generate very powerful and deep meanings within us.

I suggest that if this interests you then you can find further reading by visiting sufian.me/keep calm

An example of an archetype representing a brand is Starbucks. They are an Explorer, Explorers want things their own way, and they are inpatient and want something exotic. The name Starbucks comes from the first mate in Moby Dick by Herman Melville.

The next time you visit a Starbucks you will see that they are full of wood and shiny metal just like a ship. The "Explorers" are typically in their early twenties, trying to discover who they are and wanting something exotic. A simple black or white coffee simply will not do. They are impatient and don't want to "take a seat" and wait to be served.

I am just touching the surface, if this interests you then investigate further, I certainly have.

You are the King, if you find something worthwhile and of interest then indulge yourself and become wiser, you will be rewarded.

This book is interactive. To access more content for free please visit www.**sufian.me/keepcalm**

Chapter 5.12 - Is this a game?

You meet someone and they ask you "what do you do?"

How do you answer now, more importantly how will you answer when you have a business?

Will you bore them with your response? Will you confuse them and drone on and on and say that is difficult to explain? Will you just tell them what you are? I am an Accountant.

It might that you are meeting someone or that they have your business card or that they are reading your website or LinkedIn profile.

So, what do you do?

Can you describe the benefits that you offer when someone has engaged with yours services in a single and quite clear sentence?

You might think that people will know what you do from either the name of your company or your job title. You are wrong and why would you take such a risk to let other people imagine what they think it is that you do?

If you are not clear about what you do and cannot communicate this then you have a major disadvantage and will probably be wasting money on any marketing that you do.

As I've already mentioned Accountants, we will use this as an example.

So, what do you do?

- Hello my name is Sufian and I am an Accountant

Not working is it, what type of Accountant? I'm a little bored and embarrassed to tell you I'm an Accountant for fear of your perception of me.

So, what do you do?

- Hello my name is Sufian and I run a firm of Accountants that specialises in providing compliance services to small businesses.

I haven't quite fallen to sleep, my eyes have glazed over. Let's try again. This time try to add some benefit to what we do.

So, what do you do?

- Hello my name is Sufian and I help small business owners to reduce their tax bills

This is getting better; I didn't need to mention that I was an Accountant; I did mention the benefit of reducing tax bills. This is good but when I find out you are an Accountant this will fall into the "so what" category.

One more time from the top please.

So, what do you do?

- Hello my name is Sufian and we help small business owners to really be able to focus on the things that matter to their business by taking care of all things financial.

This shows a benefit and an understanding to my target market. I could make it more succinct or I could expand on this, depending on the circumstances and the context.

Write down your answer to the question: So, what do you do?

Keep refining it until you are comfortable that you it accurately depicts what you are about and you are proud to say it. See the response you get from people, if it isn't working and you have chosen the correct customer niche, and then refine it.

This has to be consistent with your identity and the "why" your business exists. It has to resonate with potential clients and it has to differentiate you in the market place.

You are free to live the life you dreamt of, you are a King.

5.13 – The changing face of PR

You have a large number of marketing channels available to you and one of those is Public relations (PR).

There is still a place for PR to help small businesses, however, not in the areas that you might think.

A PR Company will tell you that they can get stories about you in the local media, newspapers, magazines and even radio. They will do this by creating some content, a story that will resonate with local people. This story will be a vehicle for your business to ride on the back of.

The newspapers, magazines etc. are all searching for interesting content for their audiences. You provide content and it is a win win scenario.

In the old days, before the Internet, PR Companies would value the PR coverage that they got for you in terms of column inches and then the cost associated with buying this kind of coverage. The best example of a person doing this today in business is without doubt Richard Branson.

The PR Company would create this free advertising for you, for a fee, and you would relate the value to the coverage you would see with your own eyes and ego in print.

There is a fundamental flaw; the advertising they are getting is broadcast interruption advertising. It is almost worthless at driving traffic for your business. The fact that there is an article about you in the local paper, so what!

There are however two clever things that you can do.

Firstly, don't pay a PR company, unless you have more than you know what to do with, or you have no skills what so ever in coming up with a story about some aspect of your business that is news worthy. The fact that you have brought out a new range, no one cares, the fact that you have made Gemma, Office Manager, no one cares.

A story would be that a range of xyz that has been creating a fashion storm in America has its launch in the UK and it happens to be with you, that's news. If Gemma started as an Apprentice and has now moved up the ladder is also a story that would be of interest.

The second thing that you can do, and this is where the real value lies, is to use the coverage you get about you or your business to act as a third party recommendation or endorsement.

Everyone else who sees the article is still under the impression that it is meaningful. This being the case you should link and upload this to your website. You should refer to it in a blog and you should have physical copies with you and framed in your office.

The fact that a local newspaper did an article on you will impress people. The first thing people do these days before they meet someone for the first time is look them up on the Internet.

A few years ago I had tried to get a meeting with an MD of a much larger company. I rang his secretary, she arranged for the meeting. When I arrived at their offices I noticed a file about me on his desk, newspaper clippings etc. I had also been on the local BBC Radio station that week.

I had credibility walking into his office. He gave me the credibility. I had the local newspaper and the BBC to thank.

It made no difference to the level of service that my company could provide, but in his mind it did. That was the value of the PR.

At the time we recorded every incoming enquiry and recorded where people had heard about us. Not a single enquiry came from the Newspaper Article or the appearance on the local radio.

What did happen was local recruitment agents contacted me as well as various publications looking to sell advertising space. Needless to say they were barking up the wrong tree.

You are the King; be aware that actions sometimes have unintended consequences.

Chapter 6

Step 6: The fundamentals will always be the same. Cash is King and here is why.

Chapter 6.0 – Cash is king

This section should provide you with food for thought with regards to a small section of finance within your business. Remember at all times that the choices you have made will either make this following section redundant or highly meaningful.

You will hear the phrase "cash is King" a great deal, but what exactly does it mean and how can you make sure that you do not fall into the same trap as millions of business owners before you?

Firstly, what is cash? For a business cash is the ability to pay liabilities as and when they are due. The wages are due this week, a supplier needs paying today; do you have sufficient cash to pay?

Often you will see the term "cash flow" used to describe the process of money flowing in and flowing out of a business. A common way of providing management information to help you manage cash flow is a "cash flow forecast".

The amount of cash you need at any given time to run your business is "working capital". I'm not an Accountant and neither in all probability are you, so that is enough technical talk for now, what does it actually mean?

It is rather a strange concept to get to grips with, but here goes.

You can run a highly profitable business and run out of cash, fail to meet your immediate liabilities and be forced out of business. On the other hand you can run a highly unprofitable business and currently have significant amounts of cash in the Bank; you will inevitably become insolvent unless something dramatically alters.

If we look at the first scenario where you are running a highly profitable business but have insufficient cash and ask the question, how did this come about? There are a number of possibilities.

- You are giving your customers more credit than you are receiving from your suppliers. This might be by agreement or by customers bending the rules and paying late. As an example you purchase widgets for £100 and sell them for £130. You pay your supplier within 30 days and your customers pay you within 30 days, only some of them don't. The ones that don't take 60 days to pay, suddenly you potentially have a shortfall in cash to pay your suppliers and therefore you cannot purchase any more stock.

- You purchased too much stock. The stock is sitting on your floor and is tying up cash. When the product is sold it will generate a profit, however for the time being it is causing a cash flow problem.

- A combination of both late payers and too much stock will have the same end result.

The big question is, how do you avoid this?

If we firstly look at the payment terms agreed with your customers. When you agree to exchange goods for money you will have a set of terms and conditions, part of these will stipulate payment terms. This is not a wish list; this is part of the terms of the trade. Your first step is to make sure, get appropriate advice, that your terms are protecting you and you are clearly communicating them.

If signatures are required for proof of delivery etc. then make sure that systems are in place to insure that these are adhered to. I will explain why later.

You are a small business, you do not have sufficient "wool on your back", a term used to describe having sufficient reserves to weather difficulties in periods of negative cash flow or periods of unprofitably.

Don't let the news fool you, there will often be stories of large companies who have posted a loss for this quarter and no some seems to be unduly panicking. They are operating in a different environment and have sufficient "wool on their backs" to survive and prosper.

If you are dealing with consumers then you should either be getting paid before delivery of service or at the actual point of delivery. If you are offering credit terms please ask yourself, why?

If you are business to consumer provider you should never be in a negative cash flow position, there are some exceptions. These exceptions tend to be big ticket items, such as double glazing, building work etc.

You are dealing with amateur buyers who are not trying to hold out payment or go bust on you.

Have your systems in place and ask for payment when it is due, if it is not forthcoming on the due date then take immediate action. Before payment is due you should have confirmed that the customer is satisfied and that they have been reminded when payment is due, either by correspondence or in person via a phone call.

The immediate action could be a phone call, a visit or a letter before action which normally gives them another 7 days to pay (find out more from your advisor).

There will still be times when consumers fail to pay. If you have exhausted everything that you could have done and I mean everything then suck it up and get on. The first times this happens to you, if it does, it will hurt and it will hurt badly. You will feel as though someone has stolen from you, because if you have done everything that you were supposed to, they in effect have stolen from you.

The pain can be made worse if the product you supply has small gross margins; you buy something for £100 and sell for £130. You will have paid your supplier at a minimum and then have to recover the £100 on other sales to recover. In some industries margins are very tight and one bad debt can wipe out a whole month's worth of trading.

You may be at the other end of the spectrum and have very high margins and be able to take it on the chin without too much discomfort.

If we look at business to business transactions these are more complicated. Often you are dealing with professional buyers, with longer term relationships and often with companies who are larger than you and who will want to dictate their terms and conditions to you.

You normally allow customers 30 days to pay and suddenly you are faced with a large company telling you that their terms are 90 days. You have a choice; walk away if this is something that you cannot afford to accept. You can get funding from your bank and there are other financial facilities that can bridge this working capital gap.

Unlike the business to consumer market the majority of business transactions will not be paid on time. If you are expecting to be paid in 30 days you are in for a big disappointed.

Other companies are going to use your goods and services as working capital. The longer they can put off paying you and other suppliers and the quicker they can get paid from their customers the more profitable they will be. They will use your money instead of taking out an overdraft with the bank. Your money is free.

What can you do? You have your systems in place to track activity, but you also have other options. A company that constantly pays you late is probably also paying other companies late, their 30 days actually means 60 days.

Make a decision on whether you want to continue supplying them, if you do then try these approaches. Contact the payments section of their accounts department and make a nuisance of yourself. Call them every day and remind them that payment has not been received. Become a priority and a pain for the person who is responsible for getting the payments sent out. Make sure that you are always top of the list of payments to be made, because you will be straight on the phone.
Speak to the customer and offer them a discount for prompt payment, this is standard practise in some industries. Your invoice for £130 will be reduced by 1% if payment is received with 14 days or 30 days.

Finally, if you can, increase your prices to cover for the cost of doing business with them.

As far as late payments are concerned there are 2 basic types of customers, those that just want to pay late and see it as some sort of game and those that never intend to pay.

We have covered the game players, now those that never intend to pay.

You see the news headlines about a large organisation that is laying thousands of staff off, maybe they have gone into administration. Behind these headlines could be hundreds of small companies that are affected.

A supply chain has been broken and sometimes within this chain are serious villains. They run businesses that grow and get large contracts and never intend to pay suppliers. It is a form of white collar mugging.

If you get caught in this you are going to have to chalk it down to experience and move on.

You may find yourself with the chance of supplying a new customer who initially places small orders and pays well within the agreed terms; they might even pay up front. Once they have got your trust they will provide you with a much larger order, maybe at the last minute and maybe with a story that a very large and well known customer has requested this or another supplier has let them down. You are so focused on fulfilling this order that you don't take time to consider the real financial implications.

You supply the goods and you never, despite your best efforts and despite the tremendous emotional investment and pain, get paid.

You have never had a letter from an administrator before and when you receive it your heart sinks, however, there is hope that you will salvage something.

A large well know company was involved, on the news you see that they are concentrating on the poor staff who worked for the failed business and whether a white knight can be found to salvage some of the business and therefore some of the jobs. You are forgotten, you are small, and you do not make the headlines.

You have heard politicians speak on how they are tough on big businesses paying suppliers within terms etc. and having codes of conduct.

You expected that large organisations would carry out due diligence on all their suppliers. How did this happen?

It is complicated and the administrator will recover any monies that it can,

156

firstly for secured creditors, you are not one of these and you have to stand in line with everybody else. They will also make sure they get paid themselves.

If the business that has failed is not too large, your customer which is not the large well known company will start up again with the same owners. This is called a "phoenix", sometimes they will have virtually the same name and they might even have the gall to contact you to see if you want to supply them.

It doesn't seem right, but it is all legal. It doesn't seem fair, yet it happens every day. A limited company and its Directors are two separate legal entities. There has to be proof that a company's Directors acted with intent to defraud. Given the failure rate of businesses there are a million more palatable probabilities that are given. If there are any cases where company Directors have been found guilty of this crime I don't know of any.

Every person I know who supplies business to business has faced this situation, and some on numerous occasions. It is not a reason to avoid business to business transactions it is simply more information to help you to take the appropriate steps so that if this does occur the impact to you is minimal.

At the end of the day you must move on or it will consume you.

Working for a large organisation there simply is no emotion attached to bad debts.

Imagine you found out that a good friend has been borrowing money from you, telling you that they were short of money, only to find out they had used your loan to have a foreign holiday. You catch them out and they apologise and by the way they cannot afford to ever pay you back, money that you were relying on and needed, how would you feel? Times this by a thousand and this is how you will feel when it happens to you in your business.

We will now follow a story about Jimmy who owns a Web Development Agency. When I met Jimmy he had grown his business to around 8 developers and had secured a number of very high profile clients. His company did excellent work and Jimmy prided himself on always delivering a tailored service to every customer.

He told me the story of a medium sized professional company that he had recently engaged with. They were either a Legal firm or Accountants, it is irrelevant.

Jimmy had a number of meetings with the client over redeveloping their existing website, to make it more current and more in line with their corporate image and aspirations. Jimmy took along a Web Developer called Anthony along to every meeting and gave the project to him.

After around six weeks of developing and re-iterations, a lot of which took place within Jimmy's company, the client contacted Jimmy and was told that they had decided not to continue with the project. Other priorities had come up and that for the foreseeable future this would not be on their radar screens.

They would pay a reasonable amount for the development that they have seen so far. Based on what they had seen they thought that it was probably about a day's worth of programming and therefore offered a sum of money.

Jimmy was shocked and tried to explain that they had been working for the past six weeks on the project and that Anthony had been almost full-time on it. The client was having none of this and stood their ground.

Jimmy decided that it wasn't worth the upset to continue to argue so he agreed to accept their payment as a final settlement.

Jimmy told me that his mistakes were not being clear on his terms and conditions, not agreeing upfront when and how he was going to invoice them and also failing to communicate how the process would work. The client had no idea of what was involved in developing a website of the complexity that they were looking for and Jimmy had failed to communicate the value that his company brought to this process. They thought that they were buying a commodity and Jimmy was providing a bespoke, luxury service.

It was an important lesson for Jimmy that he will never repeat again.

In the corporate world you have been playing by the Marquess of Queensbury rules, depending on the market you are entering you might be surprised to find that some of the businesses prefer street fighting. Do not expect to enter a market and alter this.

Before I entered the world of small business I had never come across people who were deliberately trying to con me out of money. I had come across employees who stole, and often saw their crime as victimless. These people tended to be very personable and charming and plausible.

Cash can only be become King if you decide to allow it to.

You have a choice of markets and customers. You decide whether to give credit or not and to whom; choose wisely and act quickly when you need to.

This book is interactive. To access more content for free please visit www.**sufian.me/keepcalm**

Chapter 6.1 - Business Plans

Before you start a business you will be asked, in most likelihood, to provide a business plan.

I don't have a great deal to say about this as you can find out from numerous sources how to create one.

I would ask the following questions.

Why am I creating a business plan? Is the plan for you to confirm that your plans have legs or is it for some other reason, such as a Bank who wants some evidence before they will consider funding you.

Is the plan to raise venture capital? If this is the case then you will almost definitely require specialist help.

Virtually every business plan that has ever been created will have these 2 common flaws.

Firstly, they will over estimate revenues. Ask any Accountant and they will tell you this, no one has a crystal ball and even long established businesses with relatively stable year on year sales cannot forecast accurately from one month to the next. You are asking yourself to predict how something that doesn't exist now will perform.

Secondly, they will underestimate costs. If you have ever owned a car you will have probably fallen into this trap. There are the obvious costs such as fuel and insurance, however the largest cost if you purchase a new car is the depreciation. Other costs such as replacing tyres, windscreen wipers, bulbs etc. will also probably pass you by.

You are left with a flawed plan, but you will have a plan and as they say some plan is better than none.

I know people who work rigidly to their business plan whilst others have never created one and are equally as successful.

You are the King; decide to plan and be prepared for the unexpected.

Chapter 7
Step 7: You need to look for the exit before you enter your business.

Chapter 7.0 – Where's the exit?

Before you start your business you should have thought about an exit strategy.

In other words, at some point in the future how will you maximise the value that you have created into something that someone else would want to pay for, if this is what you are planning to do.

Most business owners do not consider this until it is too late. They often get a shock and realise that their precious business is not worth anywhere near what they thought it might be and in some cases it is worth nothing to someone else.

Remember that price is what you pay for something. You will realise in setting prices for your own goods and services that there are no rules. There are limits to what markets and customers will pay, but there are no rules. Value on the other hand is what you get.

If you are planning to build up a business and then sell it and move on to something else then you will operate and think about your business differently than a business that you never intend to sell and maybe pass on to your children.

If you want to sell your business then a prospective buyer has to either imagine that they can run your business or that they can put a manager in place to run it for them.

This means that you will have to have documented systems and procedures in place and that you yourself must not be an integral part of the business. You might decide to hire plant & machinery rather than outlay capital expenditure and purchase, you may decide to search out for larger contracts with higher profile clients that deliver smaller margins but leave the door open to expand sales if more effort was focused on developing these relationships.

You might sign a contract to service customers over a number of years and tie them in to show that you have continuity of sales and you have removed some of the risk of sales drying up.

If you have intellectual rights that you have protected you might consider licensing or selling these.

Another option is to develop your business in such a way that you are able to franchise the business. There are always people out there looking to start a business that has a proven track record and therefore reduced risk.

Seek advice from the professionals around you; they will have vast experience of business owners who have been in your position, some who have been highly successful at selling whilst others will no doubt prove to be cautionary tales.

You are the King; if you decide to pass on your crown you can always find other kingdoms to rule.

This book is interactive. To access more content for free please visit www.**sufian.me/keepcalm**

www.ingramcontent.com/pod-product-compliance
Lightning Source LLC
Chambersburg PA
CBHW051703170526
45167CB00002B/510